About the Author

B.E. Thompson is a Masters graduate in Coaching Psychology with background experience within the Community Justice Field. Following her journey to achieve her first BA Degree in Criminal Justice to be a Probation Officer, she managed the high risk Intensive programme in the Youth Offending Team then went onto senior management within the housing sector. This role came to an end following her additional role as a carer. B.E Thompson is also a member of her local church where she has spent some time developing and co-ordinating the Prayer Ministry Team, she is also a Tutor and a Work Style Coach and has recently become a CEO and founder of her recruitment service set up to coach, advise and provide support on image and style with the aim to empower individuals and groups seeking employment.

Dedication

I would like to dedicate this book to my 2 children who are now amazing strong adults and my grandchild, to encourage them to maintain their strength by making positive choices, never give up on their dreams and aspirations and learn from mistakes. Lastly always seek to adopt healthy behaviours and habits to be the best version of themselves they can be.

B.E. Thompson

THROUGH WITHERED WEEDS FLOWERS BLOOM

AUSTIN MACAULEY PUBLISHERS™

LONDON • CAMBRIDGE • NEW YORK • SHARJAH

A CIP catalogue record for this title is available from the British Library.

ISBN 9781398408876 (Paperback)
ISBN 9781398408883 (Hardback)
ISBN 9781398404267 (ePub e-book)
ISBN 9781398408890 (Audiobook)

www.austinmacauley.com

First Published (2021)
Austin Macauley Publishers Ltd
25 Canada Square
Canary Wharf
London
E14 5LQ

Acknowledgements

I first would like to thank God for his grace, guidance, and his continued patience with me along my life journey.

I would like to thank Bishop TD Jakes and his Ministry for their constructive teaching and mentoring during my journey writing this book.

I would also like to thank Joyce Meyer Ministries who through her story helped me eliminate shame from my life, build resilience, and transform my pain into a place of power.

FOREWORD

Karen was fifteen when she was placed on Probation. In those days Probation dealt with under 18s. The court placed her on a Supervision Order. To be honest, I don't know what they wanted supervised but they probably didn't know what else to do.

When the order finished I didn't see Karen for thirty five years, except once after perhaps ten years when she came to my office to ask how to become a probation officer. I told her how it generally happened and she went away. Then, twenty five years later, she made contact again and asked me to write this foreword.

I had heard nothing of her meanwhile and have no way of substantiating what she has written. But nor would I want to. I don't think anyone who reads this book would question the authenticity of its horror, brutality and later redemption.

Thirty five years so, Karen was a lost child. She was also a lost young woman. I never knew about all the terrible things that had happened or would happen to her but I knew enough to realise that she had not been treated right.

If you want them to act with respect, including to themselves, people must be treated with respect. Karen did not even have her own bed. She was not fed regularly. Her family did not supervise her homework, her clothes or her friends. Having no affection at all at home, she sought it elsewhere. It was most easily available in the wrong places.

But there is something which Karen herself puts her finger on. She had not been listened to. Being listened to suggests that you are worth listening to. It brings self-respect and self-confidence. When a child says, "I want to be an artist" you don't say "you can't draw a straight line"; you say, " where's the art college?" The child who is believed In will come to believe in herself.

Then there is nurture. You can't always be verbally nurturing; it would put people right off. Sharing a bag of nuts and raisins is just as good (she was lucky it wasn't sunflower seeds incidentally). I was vaguely aware she was hungry. So was she. We ate them together.

Writing this memoir has enabled Karen to examine her past and see things as they really were. Then she could understand them and finally put them behind her. She says it has been healing. The book may also help others in the same situation. She has achieved a great deal despite horrifying treatment at home and elsewhere. You can do it too.

Jeremy Cameron
April 2020

(Jeremy is now a well-known author)

Earth

"Murphy, no, stop. Ooh stop Murphy." Lion ford Murphy was beating my mother yet again. She always screamed at him to stop and I could hear the thuds and furniture trembling from the power of his blows to her body. There was shouting and screaming that was muffled as I moved further and further away from what I was scared to see. I once saw Lion beat her and lent on her leg as if trying to break it. One Sunday when we were getting ready for church my mother was doing her hair in the mirror and he smashed her face into it, there was blood. This was a regular thing in my household growing up as a child, my parents always argued and never seemed to like each other much. I never saw them hug or kiss or show any affection towards each other.

One late evening my mother and I walked out of the house because she did not want to sleep in the same bed as Lion, this was also a regular pattern for my mother, and she often would leave sometimes in the dead of the night with my two older sister's, brother and I. We would stay at friends' homes or even sometimes we would stay with kind strangers that took pity when hearing my mother's plight. On this particular night I remember my mother left very late in the evening but she only took me with her on this occasion, probably because my sisters shared a room and my brother had his own room so she had no choice to bring me because I slept in my parents room. On other occasions I would be sent to sleep with my sisters but would assume this would happen when they were probably getting on.

I remember us walking down the street on this particular night, it was very cold, and I had to run in order to keep up with my mother as she always walked at a very fast pace.

We arrived at a building, I remember men in black uniforms. They showed us to a room and gave us some blankets, I remember it being very cold. I now know this to be the local Police Station, they allowed us to sleep in one of their police cells. My mother decided to leave after a short while and thanked them as she walked out. We walked back to our house, I remember feeling really cold, my feet and hands were numb, not to mention how tired I was. My mother stood at the bottom of the stairs, she seemed scared, "Murphy, (she called Lion-ford Murphy) it's not fair for Karen to be out at this late time, she is cold and tired can she come up and get some sleep" "Come up Kaz" Lion replied, calling me to come up to bed. I did not really want to leave my mother, where would she go? However, I was also so happy to be able to be in a warm bed. I remember climbing the stairs, they seemed really big as I took the strides with my small legs, and it felt like I was climbing a mountain. I re-call getting into the bed and it being really warm, I was looking forward to finally being comfortable.

However, that was not to be the case. Lion climbed on top of me and molested me, I re-call it hurting me but not as much as it should have. Could this have happened before? He ejaculated and complained about the mess whilst giving me a cloth to wipe myself. I don't remember sleeping that night. My childhood was never to be the same again. I did not tell anyone what happened for many years, I kept the secret. Although, I knew it was wrong I did not mind it happening again, you see, it was the only time I ever remember having any physical contact with Lion or anyone else in my family. I did not understand that it was sexual, I did not know what all that meant.

But somehow I knew it was wrong and that people should not know. How did I know at such a young age? I do believe now that at the time God used one of his angels to plant that 'wrong' feeling inside of me because it made all the difference to the rest of my life's journey.

Soil

This chapter looks at the next stage of my life during my early school years. It was around 1975 when I started Infant Primary School. I remember playing in the Wendy house in the classroom, it had a telephone, a wig, some hats and clothes. I enjoyed playing 'dress-up' and always looked forward to playing with other children and being the one to wear the wig. It was at this point I knew I would love being at school. My first teacher was an old woman who had white hair and wore glasses, she was also very strict and never seemed to smile much. I especially liked the school dinners. I can still re-call the smell of potatoes and lamb being cooked as we learnt in the classrooms. I would always keep my dinner ticket safe in my purse belt so I did not lose it.

At playtime we had a tuck shop and I liked to buy the mojo sweets but we would be encouraged to get nuts and raisins or apple slices. Food in school was much healthier back then, you would get a full cooked meal that had taste. There was a wired gate that separated the infants from the juniors, my older siblings were in that part of the school, but I never remember speaking to them much, not like the other children who spoke to their older siblings through the gates. I would walk to and from school by myself, I think my brother was meant to walk with me but he was either ahead or nowhere to be seen but that did not bother me, I really liked school and was excited about being with other children my age. I liked it so much I would often go to friends' houses after school to continue to play. Most children were not allowed to play out, but I would sometimes be invited in to their homes.

My family never came looking for me or asked where I was. I could always slip out at any time without any monitoring of where I was or who I was with. I know now that this was a serious case of child neglect but at the time it never really bothered me because it meant I could play with other children anytime I wanted to. Children rarely ever knocked for me or came to my house, I would always go and seek others which meant sometimes having to wait outside their house for them to be available. I now understand that my way of interacting with my new found friends was not appropriate to my age group, we were too young to be walking about the streets knocking on doors that were like three-four blocks away from their own home but I did not know this at the time.

Home for me was not a place I enjoyed, my sisters would be doing their own thing, my eldest liked listening to music (good music by today's standards.) and rocking to the music, she rocked to and fro so much there would be a dent in the middle of the mattress were she rocked for hours. Sometimes I would lie down on the bed because her rocking gave me comfort. My other sister was mostly out with friends and so I do not remember her much growing up. My brother was very competitive so played a lot of sport, he would get medals for different sports. We would play sometimes, things like table tennis or cricket where I would sometimes win but that was only because he was so good and that helped me improve. I'm not sure he realized that because he would often get upset if I won, this brought me pleasure to win sometimes.

My mother liked going to church this was the only time she really interacted with me, I had to get up really early on Sundays to go to church with her, she would clean the hall in preparation for the church. I did not understand why she would always do this because they never thanked her, instead they would call her names and laughed at her, once the pastor even shouted at her to get out and threw her belonging towards the door. They had a church van that picked people up and dropped them off, we rarely got this service we always walked or got the bus and watched as they all passed us at the bus stop. This made me very sad as a child, I did not understand why we were treated differently and so badly, I felt sorry for my mother.

My mother had a mental illness, they diagnosed her as a paranoid schizophrenic, I did not know much about it at the time, but I understood she heard voices and at times behaved in a bizarre way. I had to sleep in her room at night so when she would be having one of her particularly bad episodes. It meant she would be up all night doing things most people would do in the day like ironing, cleaning, talking to herself or arguing with me and criticizing me, she would often pray and sing very loudly whilst sometimes telling me to get up and pray.

Most evenings, probably about four nights per week, she would decide to go to evening church meetings, I did not like going but had to, it was not nice having to get the bus late at night. I never liked going, I got nothing from this, no one ever spoke to me and I did not participate, it was not very child-friendly. I mostly slept or would lie down because I was so tired. These were my first experiences of 'church folk' and what was supposed to be Christianity.

In Sunday school I would learn about how good God was and how much he loved me and everyone else in the world but I definitely did not see this from my early experience with my mother or the church. There was a definite conflict in how I viewed God. My mother was sectioned under the Mental Health Act quite a few times, I would often arrive home from school and be told 'mum is in hospital' I remember visiting her, she always seemed so tired but would be very calm which was very different from her constant criticism and shouting. She was a very angry women towards my siblings and I, but she was always so nice to her church friends or people outside the family, she was like two different people but I believe this was because she was sick with low family values.

My mother often told me I would die young and would not live for very long. Later on in life when I asked her why she always told me this as a child, she said she meant I would die and become a Christian which I think she would have explained it in this way, if that is what she thought. My mother was cruel and had a very cruel tongue, as a child her words got me thinking about death when my life was only just starting. I suppose the good news is, I never believed her... It's funny but I learnt never to believe anything she said, whenever she said something negative to me or about me (which was very often.) I would always think *No. I'm not that.* I always believed myself to be much more, I always wished one day she would be kind. I would daydream about being in a different family with people who loved me and cared about me and that's probably why I would often go to people's homes, it was nice to feel like part of their family at times, even if it was for a short while.

During my infant and primary years, I was very welcoming to new children in the school and would always befriend them by knocking for them in the morning on my way to school or after school or at the weekend to come out to play or I would play in their homes. This is why most of the people I went to school with that were new to the area would say I was their first friend. I believe I got something very positive out of it and so did they. I did this for most of my school years. It was important to me because I did not feel wanted at all at home and most of my friend's parents were kind so being friends with those who were new to the area filled a purpose for us all.

I would always pretend to have cousins and grandparents and aunts who would visit but the truth was the only family was Lion's family and they never visited. I had no-one but I did not let this bother me at the time because it was the 'norm' but pretending I had a close knit family made me feel better, I did not like pity. I learnt from a very early age to create my home environment that mirrored others so that I did not look different, but I longed to be able to have a 'normal' home life, one that was similar to my peers. I actively sought friends, I played out all day every day, especially in the school holidays. Lion worked nights on British Rail so slept a lot during the day, if he worked days, he would mostly come home angry and end up beating either my mother or my other siblings so being at school was more comforting. During the early seventies about 1976-77 my mother left the house (again) this time we ended up in a hostel that was down the road.

It was a huge hostel with a lot of rooms filled with what looked like working class families from different cultural backgrounds and all who were homeless. We had double rooms. I think because there were five of us, but I loved this place. I think I loved it so much because I did not have to be around the family who consistently dismissed my existence, I could now interact and spend most of my time with other residents and not have to leave home to do this because we were all under one roof. However, this did not come without a downside. As mentioned, this hostel probably housed troubled families, I'm not sure what the criteria would have been but it was the 70s and by the issues my family had faced I can only assume that the families that lived there must have had their own issues too. I played regularly with the other children, most of them older boys. The girls that lived there mostly stayed in their rooms and did not play around the hostel grounds like I did, I was a bit of a tom boy. One day the boys played an operation game and asked me to be the patient, they sexually abused me during this time, it happened again whilst we were behind the large silver bins at the front of the hostel. My sister Joan came out to put something in the bin and caught them abusing me. I recall her face in shock, she ran in and told my family and called me dirty. I ran away and hid for a few hours ashamed and embarrassed. I was scared to go back to the room because I thought I was going to get into trouble, but nobody said anything to me when I returned. I would have been roughly 6 years old and these boys were older than me, I had no protection, but I was used to this. I was always made to feel responsible and at fault from a very young age so it did not really affect me at the time as much as it should have. I continued to play and interact with families, fortunately most people were quite nice. I did not miss my other house at all, I did not even visit there…

I would leave from the hostel in the mornings and go to school which was about a ten-fifteen minute walk but when I got 'home' I was back to doing what I did best, knocking on doors for children to play out or meeting in the hall with other children. I spent most of the time in people's rooms or playing on a building site that was close by. I remember once I was playing on this site and a nail went through my foot. I had to attend the hospital for them to remove the nail, it was extremely painful.

I loved the hostel environment because it allowed me to play and interact with children who lived under the same roof, I did not have to go too far anymore. I liked it so much I stopped going to school. I was roughly age six or seven and pretended to leave for school but stayed in the hostel visiting people in the different rooms whilst keeping out of sight from my mother or anyone that might tell her. I kept this up for some time, several days maybe more, but one day my mother came into the wash room where I was, not sure why I was in there but when she came in I quickly hid in a corner but she saw me and shouted, asking why I was not in school. Of course she marched me off to school where they informed her that I had not attended school for some time.

When they asked me why I did not attend school, I could not give an answer. However, in hindsight I do think leaving the unhealthy environment I was familiar with and living in a hostel with equally unhealthy people may have impacted on my behaviour but I found what I perceived as much happiness in the hostel and felt sad when we had to leave and move back to the family home.

Seeds

I must have moved back to the house in 1978 because I recall this is the year Lion had to leave the house following a very serious incident where he broke my sister's arm whilst beating her. I remember my eldest sister taking me to visit her in a children's home. I remember thinking how lucky she was to be living out of the house with all that support and people she could talk to. In hindsight, I can imagine this was a very painful time for us all, but I was pleased to see my sister and to know she was safe. The day Lion had to leave, I remember he was crying, I had never seen him cry but he did on this occasion, it was a howling type wailing scene which is why it is so vivid to mind, he looked pitiful. It seemed he blamed my mother for making them put him out of the house. My understanding is my mother had no choice because the authorities said he would not be able to stay in the house any longer due to his violence and if my mother took him back, she would lose us all and also her home. I wonder, if my mother did not have this alternative maybe she would have stayed with him, given the choice as she always returned following his violence. I believe the ultimatum that was given by the authorities probably saved us from further physical and sexual abuse, although I was to continue to experience mental and emotional abuse through neglect. I do believe there were some good seeds but also some bad seeds at this point. The next four mini chapters will explore the good seeds.

Sports

I was now in the junior part of school and was enjoying every minute of it. We had different activities and I was friends with Madeline, who was my age. I started to learn to play netball and here I found my passion for a specific sport. I made the team and played centre position, Madeline was also in the team, so we had a lot in common, she became my best friend. We would always sing Lovers Rock songs by Jean Adembambo, Carol Thompson and Janet Kay during break time or on the coach going on school trips. We had older siblings similar in age, so we had access to these songs from listening to them play the records. We also would sing songs from the Disco 45 song book which had lyrics.

Our netball coach was really nice and always encouraged us to be the best we could be. I loved netball, this was very nurturing and helped me validate my skills and talents. I was one of the shortest on the team but was the fastest. My Centre position meant I could go in all areas of the game except the circle where the shooters scored. I worked very closely with another friend called Jo-Jo. She was the Wing Attack and was very good and fast so we were able to keep up with each other. I would sometimes go to her house to play at the weekends or in the school holidays. Our netball team was very good and when we played other schools we would usually win. On a few occasions we would get to semi-finals but unfortunately a stronger team would always beat us to the cup...

I still love netball and always will. I loved school. Juniors was my favourite because I had netball and had my first experience of being part of a team and I loved it. I also liked that I was good at something which allowed me to feel a sense of purpose and empowerment. I practiced netball every day and sometimes all day in my garden at the weekend. I secretly wished I had a shooting (goal attack) position because I was frustrated that whilst I would do all the work with the team as Centre position, the shooters would then fail to score. I always think if we had better shooters, we would win the tournaments and bring home the cups. I recall there being a hole in the roof of our shed in the garden and so I would use this as the shooting net and pretend that I was the shooter but to be frank I was not very good at shooting either...

I remember the first time we received our netball kit which was green and yellow, I was so proud. We all looked so good. I had never felt like this before, I think this was the first time I felt self-worth, this increased my confidence and I started to believe in myself, not realizing this feeling would stay with me for the rest of my life regardless of what or where life's journey would take me. I quickly realized my skills in physical activities, which meant I also competed in the school sports day. I was always featured in the 100 meters race but sadly always came about third or fourth. I think one year I did come second which made me very proud, but the relay was where I would always get my gold medal, I would usually start the relay or be second to take the baton.

No family member ever attended as spectators, but I became used to this, in fact I convinced myself to prefer this because the contrast was so different, I did not want any of my family to spoil or take away the happiness I had within school. Although, I would play a lot of sports with my brother Hudson at home. Hudson was very good at sport, I believe he may have also got his confidence and self -identity through this channel so we had this in common. We would play many ball games.

Hudson was extremely competitive but because he was so good, he would help me to improve my skills which meant sometimes (not often) I would win. I would gloat and tease him but really, he was my teacher in sports. Hudson helped me to become competitive, but I was never a sore loser because I knew he was a lot better than me.

Resourceful – Stock Room

During my junior years I was chosen to deliver stationery to the classes that were running low on supplies. This was a great job because firstly it got me out of the classroom for the entire morning or afternoon (well I took my time delivering which meant it took that long.) but mostly I can reflect back and realize I learnt to organize and prioritize whilst being efficient. I would sort through all the teachers' requests and go to the stock room and collect the supplies. I would then organize each individual request and deliver the stationery to the individual classrooms. I loved this. It also helped build my confidence and it built a sense of trust between me and the teachers, they even allocated me a helper. One of my favourite times in the classroom was reading story books so I always made sure to do my stock room job after the reading session. My favourite book was *The Lion, The Witch and The Wardrobe*, it took me off into a fantasy that was so exciting. I also liked *Gobbolino the Witch's Cat*, this was a book about a cat that had a sister named Sootica and he went on many exciting adventures, it had nothing to do with witches at all. I liked the book so much at the time that when we got two cats, I named them Gobbolino and Sootica.

Drama

In our school we had to annually audition for the school Christmas play. I would always audition and always get a part, usually a small part but I enjoyed being involved in the whole production, this included dress rehearsals. I also played the violin for a short time. My eldest sister Carole took me to the musical instrument supply shop to collect my violin. I had to practice with others at dinner time but because I did not practice at home, I did not play this instrument for very long. I did find it interesting, however, did not get much encouragement. I liked being part of the school play because it meant being with others and knowing when it was my turn. I remember being petrified on the nights of the play worried I might get it wrong or make a mistake, but it was always ok and a great adrenalin rush, I could not wait to do it again. I did not ever get permission to attend because my mother would always say no but nobody ever really checked where I was or who I was with, so I was able to get away with it. I would not get back home until after dark but would say if anyone asked that I was at the school helping with the play. It was at that point that I knew I enjoyed drama and once I got to secondary school, I always looked forward to drama classes as it was now part of the curriculum subjects.

Music – Records

Oh Yes. My music, I loved music. I quickly learnt from a young age that I enjoyed music because my eldest sister Carole would always play music. Lion bought her a record player and she always bought records, she also had Lion's records, the old reggae albums by Delroy Wilson, Matumbi, Derrick Harriot, The paragons, The Heptones and Maytals. These and many more were part of Lion's collection that my sister inherited when he left our home. I would sit and listen to these records with my sister most days. I enjoyed a lot of her own records which consisted of lover's rock, soul and reggae. I mostly liked Savanah, Phyllis Hyman and Quincy Jones, Pieces of a Dream, Evelyn Champagne King and Al Jearau. My love for music definitely was influenced by my sister and I still love those artists today. As I became more and more interested in music as a child, I started to purchase my own records. There was a record shop at the end of our road on the corner. I couldn't even see over the counter but I knew what records I wanted to buy. Most of my purchases were pop records, the ones in the charts. I remember buying Shalamar, The Stranglers, Bucks Fizz, Mary Jane girls and Mamma Used To Say by Junior. I would take my records with me as I knocked for some of my friends, and if allowed I would let them play my records on their player system. I suppose I was a bit of a kiddie DJ as this was like a resource to help me enjoy my time when visiting others. I believe music was comforting and healing for me, I would imagine myself singing on the stage but sadly this was not a gift I had.

Brigade

Oh how I enjoyed Girls Brigade... Another outlet, another environment that allowed me to be myself but also to explore my interests and aspirations at that time in my young life. I would attend GB on Tuesday evenings, we had to pay subs at the beginning, again my mother would never agree to me attending so I would attend without her knowledge and like always no one would check where I was, so I was always home free. (Luckily, I was interested in positive things where I was safe) We had a great tuck shop that I would attend at the end. I would do all sorts of activities such as games, singing, dancing, drama and playing instruments. We had hats that we would sew our badges on, badges we received for participating well in activities, my aim was to gain as many badges as possible but only managed to get a few. We would always say a prayer:

'The grace of our Lord Jesus Christ, and the love of God, and the fellowship of the Holy Spirit be with us all, evermore. Amen'

GB had a religious ethos. Madeline lived a few doors away from the GB leader, I think her mother put in a good word for me to be able to join, if I attended by myself, I don't think I would have been allowed to join. I participated in the annual showcase every year and thoroughly enjoyed doing that, I also learned to play the drums. The drums was very exciting, there was a parade around the local streets on a Sunday and this would involve those who played the trombone, trumpet and drums. I learnt to play the drums really well and of course my best friend Madeline was also in attendance. I could not attend Sunday service which was at the local church where GB was held. This meant that all the lessons of playing the drums were not utilized as well as they could have been.

I would sometimes see the procession pass by my house and see the formation and everyone in their uniforms marching in a drill style way, the drummers were especially my favourite as I knew all of the beats but was never allowed to join in with this, this made me sad. I was also never allowed to go camping but I did attend a great showcase where we performed at the Royal Albert Hall. Both Girls Brigade and Boys Brigade participated, I am not too sure what the boys were performing but the GB delivered either a ball type formation or with ropes. I was one of the ball formations. This was my biggest event at this time and I remember being as nervous as there was a large audience, many of them being parents and families of the children taking part, my mother did not know I was even there but I remember it so clearly, it was exciting and I had a great time. All the group had to do was bounce the ball a few times, but it was exhilarating.

These four areas highlighted had a powerful influence on my childhood, I am able to see this being played out in my life as an adult because I still have the motivation and confidence to try new things with a great sense of resilience and determination.

Fertilization

This chapter is about conception as this was a time in my life that I started to explore and acknowledge emotions. It was the summer of 1980 and I was attending my last summer program at Primary School. I always enjoyed summer school because again, it meant I could spend time outside of my home in an environment that was safe and enjoyable. We played a lot of team games, made arts and crafts, learnt in a fun way by competing in quizzes and playing board games. I mostly liked the lunches and the trips out to different places. I was very small for my age and looked a lot younger than most of my peers. I remember we learnt the Green Cross Code and the Police came into assembly to talk to us about not speaking to strangers using a video called, 'Stranger Danger' "just say no to strangers" that was the theme and tagline.

This helped me and saved me from what could have been serious harm because on the same day that we had such a positive assembly, a white man with greasy hair in a car stopped by the road curb as I was walking home from school and he asked me if I wanted a lift home. I remembered what was said that day in school and shook my head to say no, he persisted that my mother had actually asked him to pick me up from school because she could not make it. I knew that was a lie because nobody ever picked me up from school. I always made my way home by myself, but he did not know that. I walked at a faster pace in order to get away from this man and he eventually drove away. That was my second time experiencing a male predator approaching me as a small child, luckily on this occasion I got away.

There was no point in telling my mother, she never responded to anything I said with concern, so I learnt very quickly not to share much with her. Summer school only lasted half the summer holidays, so I had to find other things to do for the last three weeks.

Lion would visit from time to time, giving us money or taking us to McDonalds. I remember begging him to buy us a video recorder, it was becoming quite popular at this point and of course that would help keep me quiet. He agreed as he mostly did which is why I was seen as spoilt. We bought a VHS Panasonic video player. I was so happy I went out and joined a video club once the video was set up. I started renting out five or six videos at a time. As mentioned, I was quite small for my age, but I was not only able to join the video club, but I took out films rated any age. My favourites were horrors, thrillers and action. Clubs would get into a lot of trouble renting those kinds of movies to children today but somehow, I was able to rent these movies time after time, I think I might have said they were for an adult.

I would ride my bike, roughly a fifteen minute ride and rent mostly certificate eighteen. I loved to watch these movies and would finish them in a few days and be back to rent out more the following days. I remember doing this for the rest of the summer, I didn't even bother to play outside during this time. I think I liked horror movies because of the thrill of it but I can no longer watch them today, maybe I am less brave than I was back then. The whole video movie world was a new culture for society and to my household, we no longer had to watch what was on TV and could video shows when not at home. It was a new age and I felt very excited about being part of this. When the movie Annie came out in the cinema, I was also very excited because me and my friends would always sing and re-enact the songs.

My neighbours at the time were twin girls my age and they were into talent shows and tap and ballet, they auditioned for the stage play Annie so because we played together quite a lot, they taught me a lot about the songs and the movie. When it was showing at the cinema I could not wait to go. I knew my mother would not allow me and most of my friends had seen it, so I decided to go by myself. I remember how excited I was, I was so brave back then because I saved my pocket money or stole money from my siblings, took the bus and travelled to the cinema. I even bought myself a hot dog and a drink. I re-call a mother and her children were sitting next to me in the theatre, so we became friendly. This was my first experience of the cinema, I was alone but made friends quite easily, so it didn't really matter, and I stayed to watch the movie about three more times as I enjoyed it that much.

My other first experience was when I had a boyfriend towards the end of the final school year, he had a twin, but they were not identical. This was my first boyfriend, Madeline said we were cute together. We never kissed, I don't even remember holding his hand, but we agreed we were an item until we weren't, which wasn't for very long. He was quiet and really shy. I wasn't that quiet but I was very shy when it came to boys that I liked. I think back then we didn't really break up we just wasn't and that was fine with me. A few years later in the summer holidays of 1983 I started going out with a boy called Neil, this relationship was a little more serious than my first relationship, and it was also an emotional roller coaster. Neil was very cute, and we were the same age. I was playing at an adventure playground in the summer of 1982, all the children used to go there and older children to late teens used to play table tennis in the centre that was based next to the playground.

My brother played table tennis there too. We were all outside talking and laughing about when a girl I knew Said "I think you and Neil would make a cute couple, do you think he is cute?"

I replied, "I don't know him. Which one is Neil?"

She called him over whilst whispering "He likes you". I remember Neil coming over with a shy smile on his face. "You alright, what's your name?"

"Karen" I replied.

"I'm Neil"

"I know" I replied quickly.

"How do you know my name?"

"My friend told me"

We spent much of time just going backward and forwards with questions and answers. I thought he was good looking, but I also felt shy and unsure about what was happening. However, from the start I knew it would be something special.

After our awkward conversation, he asked me where I lived, I told him, and he offered to walk me home. As we walked, we talked and the conversation seemed to be less awkward, maybe because we were not surrounded by all the others watching us to see if we were going to hit it off. Neil walked me all the way home and we talked for a bit and he asked me what school I went to, so I told him, he went to a boy's school on the other side of the borough. I quickly said I had to go and went in. I often went to the playground where I would see him and he would walk me home, we became a more established couple over several weeks. Neil was a bit of a 'bad boy' because he smoked as I could smell this on his breath every time we kissed after he walked me home. We done this for a year before things became more intimate. I started to enjoy being with Neil because I could speak about anything to him. I would always arrange to meet with him but one day when I attended the playground I was standing around when an awful traumatic incident happened. A boy used a catapult to fire a large bit of metal at people walking past, and as I tried to move away, I was struck in my left eye.

All I remember was I felt dizzy and collapsed. I was rushed to the local hospital where they performed emergency surgery on my eye in order to save it. However, my retina was completely destroyed and they were unable to save the sight in my eye. I remember waking up to people around my bed asking me questions about my eye and if I knew what had happened, but I didn't at the time. I spent the rest of the summer holidays in hospital, I was on a ward full of elderly people that all had eye problems. I am not sure why I was never put in the children's ward. I do not remember seeing my mother or any of my family much, but this was the start of my painful journey with my eye problems that are still ongoing today but thank God I have had nine operations and some very good consultants over the years.

The year following my eye injury I developed a cataract in my left eye so was admitted to hospital again to have it removed. At this time I was still dating Neil and our relationship grew. I found out it was actually his older brother who fired the catapult that injured my eye because he eventually admitted the truth to my mother after trying to pin the blame on another boy. Neil visited what felt like every other day whilst I was in hospital for two weeks. It was nice to have someone who gave me attention because I never really got any of this at home, only from Lion who abused my trust. Neil was handsome, a little taller than me, fair skinned and slim. He also had a good sense of humour and was extremely popular. It was very flattering that he would like me because I was not used to going out with the popular boys (not yet anyway.) Neil would come and see me at my school, which meant he was bunking from his own, but I did not think of it like this at the time. He would send someone to call me to the gates and I was of course flattered by this.

I always enjoyed school so did not think of bunking off especially after the trouble it caused when I did it in the infants. All of this was to change drastically, and it was not entirely my fault. One afternoon whilst in a Geography lesson (which I always found boring) we were left to our own devices as the teacher was out of the room. One of the other pupils was being teased but I was not involved in this. The teacher came back to the room and targeted me, she began shouting and told me to leave the room. When I went outside, she followed me and physically abused me, I asked her to stop hitting me and was moving away from her, but she continued to aggressively poke and hit me in my chest whilst saying very horrible things about me and my family.

I was extremely angry and upset so eventually I hit her back and we began fighting, she pulled my hair and fought with me by pulling me to the ground whilst kicking me and punching me. The classroom door swung open with the two of us falling to the floor fighting in front of the class. Although I was upset, I was also extremely frightened by what had happened. I got up and was in complete tears. This teacher told me to go back to my seat in the classroom, I thought this was a strange request after what she did to me. I refused and told her I was going home and would never come back to the school... I ran all the way home in floods of tears and feeling distraught.

My mother was at home at the time, she responded concerned to my surprise and she believed me. I think that this was also the first time that I had ever ran to her with a problem, so she knew it had to be true.

My mother went up to the school and told off the headmaster while we were in the office, I was surprised he apologized to her. Although, he said he was unable to take me back in the school because he had to make an example of me, he would give me a glowing report.

My mother did not fight hard enough. I remember sitting there unsure why I had to leave the school. A teacher had targeted me and physically assaulted and abused me with witnesses and nothing happened to her... It was easy for her to do this and get away with it because she was the teacher and I was from a poor working class family. I was devastated.

I ended up going to an all girl's school where I already knew a few of the pupils and the boy's school that my boyfriend went to was across the road. I pretended that it was what I wanted anyway so that I could be close to my friends. I stopped caring about school at this point and started to bunk school with Neil. I even started to smoke. Whilst I was at school one afternoon during lessons I was called out of the classroom and told I had a visitor. When I stepped outside in the corridor, I saw the teacher that abused me with her husband as she introduced me to him, she asked me how I was. I was fuming, I thought *how dare this woman visit me after she attacked me and got me expelled*. I do believe upon reflection that she must have been feeling very guilty for what she had done which is why she made the visit, I found it very intimidating and uncomfortable that this bully was still able to gain access to me. I started hanging out more with Neil and his friends and we became closer, I shared the sexual abuse I experienced as a small child with him, he was very supportive and understanding which came as a surprise because we were so young and these issues were taboo back then. However, we only spoke about it once and then it was never mentioned again. I also told him about the teacher who assaulted me, he stated he believed me because I had no reason to lie. I began smoking regularly and staying out later and later.

My mother did not ever come looking for me but would always chastise me when I got home by saying, "so many young girls walk the street late at night and get attacked", and she would say 'how come you don't get attacked'. There it was again, her hoping something bad would happen to me or maybe she was trying to frighten me into staying at home, it made me stay out more. I eventually started sleeping at Neil's house or wherever we went as long as I was with him, I felt safe. We also started having unprotected sex which led to my first pregnancy at fifteen years old... I was also offending, shoplifting clothes mostly, only so that I had something to wear out.

One day I was out at the adventure playground near the estate and my friend Claire, who was a bit of a trouble maker, had started a fight with a woman but I did not know exactly what had happened. As I arrived I was told that Claire was in a fight and needed my help. I was always very loyal to my friends, so I ran towards the fight and helped my friend as this woman was beating her up. We both were able to overpower her We both ran away after but later on that night the Police came and arrested us both for assault. This was the second time I had been in a police cell and it was frightening, they just threw us into a van. I am sure the cell was the same one I had slept in with my mother when I was a toddler but can't be sure, it was certainly the same police station.

When they released us on bail, I found out that Claire had picked a fight with this innocent woman that was at the park. I realized that I was now involved. Claire's mother managed to get a solicitor and she asked my mother to let him represent both of us.

My mother agreed to this, the solicitor told me what to say and I told the story just as he advised on the stand at Court after pleading not guilty.

However, when Claire took the stand she began to cry and stated she could not lie to the Court. This behaviour made it look like I was the bad one who had started the fight and she was innocent when it was the other way around. I realized her and her mother had set me up, I was fuming... I received a one year Probation Order which meant I had to see my Probation Officer once a week. His name was Jeremy Cameron and he changed my life. Little did I know at the time that the Probation order was a great blessing in disguise and what someone wanted to do to hurt me, God managed to turn it around for my good.

Sunlight

I went to see my Probation Officer once a week at his office and he would make a home visit at least once a month. I would normally go to his office with friends waiting for me outside, but it was the home visits that were the most helpful. He was able to see how I lived, my mother never liked him, if she could stop him from attending, I think she would have, and she even accused me of having an affair with him.

Mr. Cameron was very nice and kind, he was the first person to ever listen to me and understood that I found life hard having to sleep in a room with my mother who was clearly very unwell. He would always bring nuts and raisins for us to share. I probably liked the home visits more because I did not have friends waiting and I could be myself. He always said that I did not behave like most of his clients and was surprised that I committed the offence, I wish I had told him the truth that I actually did not it was Claire. However, I think he knew I didn't by the way he was always helpful and ready to listen. I fell pregnant in the summer of 1985, but I did not want to keep the baby, I was very sick and was bed bound. I thought I was going to die because I would vomit consistently. I lost a lot of weight and no one knew why this was happening. I later found out I had a cyst on my ovary which was causing me to vomit when pregnant.

Upon reflection I do believe I may have had Hyperemesis Gravidarum (HG), which causes excessive sickness during pregnancy. Mr. Cameron managed to arrange for me to go to the hospital for a termination. I was grateful for this and have no regrets. However, upon reflection, I realize that life is a precious gift from God and so my option today would be to choose life but at the time I was young scared and very sick. Neil was not very happy, but he acted like it did not matter so he did not give me any problems, we were young. Following the termination I started to feel well again and was out and about soon after, but me and Neil drifted apart after this.

I heard several months later Neil got into a fight with an older guy and ended up stabbing him. He was then sentenced to three years imprisonment. I was sad because I had felt I had lost a good friend, I would write to him regularly, but life does go on. My Probation Officer also managed to get me a job with the Youth Training Scheme and also a place at a hostel. It was a lovely room, my very first room and I was overjoyed. I moved in swiftly, unfortunately it was short lived because I was seeing an older guy by this time and would sometimes sneak him in, or I would sleep out with him.

A girl who lived in the room adjacent to mine reported me to the office manager, I also once saw her try to access my bedroom via the balcony when she thought I was not in. Nobody liked her and I found out why, she told lies about me because she was jealous of the friendships I made in and out of the house and wanted my room because it was a nicer room with a balcony. I was subsequently evicted because of her. I reluctantly moved back home but was never there.

Mr Cameron eventually found me another hostel, this one was better without any office workers and it was much nicer. Again I was so happy and relieved. It was my second room and I valued it. It was a brand new 5 bed house, I got the first pick and the largest room, and I kept it clean and got on well with the other ladies who were all older than me. We had a lot of fun, we would go shopping together, cook together and rave together. They were like family and we looked out for each other like sisters. Anna was the one who liked to cook, and she could do this very well even taught me a few things.

Gina was funny and would always make me laugh. Jill was from Liverpool, she was always very friendly and also made me laugh. This was one of the happiest times of my life, I felt freedom and I had a space of my own, it was a great feeling of achievement. I also found a job, I started working in a Nursery and enjoyed this, and this is where I found my passion for working with children. I worked at a Montessori Nursery and started in the baby room, then to the middle room and lastly with the pre-school children.

I was seeing a guy called James, he lived in South London, he seemed nice and was always very attentive, paying for my cab fares home to East London, always wanting to buy me things, he agreed with everything I said, he was a bit boring but saw himself as a bit of a gangster... He would talk about knowing all the bad gangster men in South London and how he would rob drugs from drug dealers. I actually met him at my cousin's birthday party. He smoked cocaine and tried to trick me into smoking this, but I told him off and was very angry that he tried that. He never offered me cocaine again. He also told me his brother had killed a man...

I am not sure why alarm bells did not go off as all of these things he talked about were red flags but part of me did not believe him and thought he was trying to impress me into thinking he was an interesting character. At this point my good friends were Janine and Jennifer and at times Mandy when she wasn't travelling. We would go to raves such as Sound Clashes, Unity Sound System mostly. We would always listen to David Radigan on the radio on a Saturday night before leaving to go out and wake up to Tony Williams on a Sunday afternoon. The sound clash scene attracted a lot of Jamaicans, we called them 'yardies'. Most of my friends were attracted to them and even started dating them but I was never that interested and was not convinced by their charm.

One evening when we went out, my friend Jennifer was being chatted up by one of these 'yardies'. He invited her back to his place, she wanted to go but not by herself. I went along with her and waited in another room, I could hear her crying, so I ran upstairs and said we need to leave. I was very assertive back then, so he let her leave and it was us two against him. As my friend was getting herself together, his brother came into the flat. He asked if he could speak with her, I asked her if that is what she wanted so I said I would wait downstairs. It all happened so quickly but the brother came into the room and raped me. I tried to push him off, but he hit me violently and I froze. I saw someone at the corner of my eye, not sure who it was. I was so angry when I left, there I was helping and protecting my so-called friend and all the time it was me that was vulnerable and in danger. I put myself at risk for someone and as a result was hurt and badly violated.

I blamed myself but I was also angry with the man who raped me but upon reflection I realized if Jennifer wanted to be with this guy I should have let her go by herself because if I did not feel safe with a guy I would not bring a friend into it, but that was the kind of person I was, protective and loyal even to my own detriment.

In this section it may be hard to know why it is described as my sunshine but do believe having my own place made a difference. Also it was a time when God used what felt like his angels to help me through probably one of the most difficult time in my life.

Germination

This chapter explores the seeds that started to grow in my life journey. The spore germination only grows when the condition is right. It was a few months later and I noticed I was feeling unwell, vomiting with bad stomach cramps. I attended the hospital where they told me that I was pregnant. At this time I was working in my first real job as a Montessori Nursery Nurse, I enjoyed this role as it meant I was working with children which was a great passion for me at the time. However, I was very, very sick. I remembered the first pregnancy and realized this sickness was not going away any time soon. I then had to leave my job due to my illness associated with my pregnancy. I began to think about the father who I believed to be James but then I was raped and then there was Pete. I had been seeing Pete for a few weeks. He was so nice, handsome and someone who I liked a lot. I remember being admitted to hospital because I was so unwell and could not keep any food or liquid in my body, so they put me on an Intravenous Drip. Whilst in hospital I remember a nurse saying to me that I should think about having an abortion, she stated they could take me downstairs and it would all be over by the following day. I have to admit this was so tempting, I felt awfully sick and with not eating or drinking anything for days I felt a little spaced out, not to mention the constant pain in my abdomen. However, I knew I wanted my baby, regardless of the circumstances so I refused her offer. I was in hospital for almost a week but needed looking after so I ended up going to live with my sister Joan.

My other sister Carole Anne by this time became mentally unwell and was not able to live in her flat anymore, she would walk about naked on the street, mostly with a coat over her but nothing else. Carole was completely broken by the sexual and physical abuse that happened to her as a child. Carole looked after me during my first pregnancy. Being the eldest child, it seems she went through the abuse first. She went through horrendous sexual abuse and physical assaults that resulted in her having a disability in her leg and foot, she ended up in supported living and stayed in that environment until she died in September 2017. Carole never made it back from the mental place she locked herself in. I know if she was well enough, she would have looked after me as she did before.

I stayed with Joan for several months during my pregnancy and she looked after me well, she also had two children of her own, so I appreciated all she did for me and felt very close to her following this. I moved back to my hostel when I was about six months pregnant and was fortunate they kept the room for me whilst I was allowed to be there. Unfortunately I was told I would have to leave before having the baby and would have to go back to my own borough to find accommodation. I was now back at the hostel and the others were pleased to see me, they said that James had been asking for me and that they had all missed me. I was happy to be back, back in my own space, I too had missed being there. I quickly settled in, but it was not long before James came to visit. I really did not want to see him as I had been seeing Pete who I preferred and really liked. Although I did let James in (which was a big mistake…), I only let him in to tell him I did not want to be with him and that I had been unwell.

I can't remember if I told him that I was pregnant because all of a sudden James pulled my letter opener from my pen holder which had a sharp edge and held it to my stomach and threatened to kill me. I was scared and confused, he seemed so nice and soft to me in the past but here I was faced with a wild animal. He accused me of taking him for a fool and that I had told people what he was like in bed. I realized he was crazy and was worried that he would really kill me... I pretended to understand and started to talk softly and nicely to him in order to calm him down. When I done this he changed and started to smile. What a sicko... He was strange and I wanted him out of my room. At first, he would not allow me to leave the room but as I continued to pretend by saying I liked him he eventually let me leave the room to use the toilet. I quickly passed a note to one of the other girls to call my sister so that her boyfriend could come and help me get him out. Upon reflection I should have called the police. Greg, my sister's boyfriend, who was always like a big brother to me, came and got him out. Greg worked as a bouncer so was familiar with the likes of James. I was so grateful to Greg and my sister for helping me. I was also very happy that I got rid of James. It was not long after I returned to the hostel when my key worker Jill asked to meet with me. At the meeting she explained that I was no longer able to stay at the hostel because of my pregnancy because they were only able to house single women, being pregnant changed my status and I was told I had to leave. Jill was really nice and stated she would help me find suitable accommodation, she worked alongside Mr Cameron and I was subsequently offered a two bedroom flat. I was extremely grateful to her, she also helped me move into the flat when the decorating was finished. Mr Cameron organised a group of people who were doing Community service to paint my flat as part of their order. I purchased the material and they done a great job.

Once again Jeremy Cameron came to the rescue and helped me. These people that had done my flat were not only learning a great trade of painting and decorating but they also done a great deed. I moved my clothes and other items for my baby into the flat following this. I had no furniture as yet, but Jill was able to help me with applications for grants to assist with buying essentials. I missed Jill and Jeremy because they were like angels sent to help me at a time I was in need and they did just that, this was the first time I received genuine support, love and care that was consistent. My experience with them changed my whole outlook on life, I knew at this point that I could achieve my goals. However, it would get harder before it got better.

Plumule Breaks Cotyledons

Germination of broad bean

Plumule emerges

Radicle continues
to grow

The summer of 1988, and my daughter was born, she weighed 6lb 4oz and had lots of hair. I was excited but also very tired. Leanne was getting up on the hour every hour for her feed and at times I was feeding her with my eyes shut, big shock to the system. I was able to spend the first month at my sisters which was helpful, but I had to get up every time to feed and look after Leanne. I was able to get carpet for my bedroom and my sister loaned me her old pram which was like a Moses basket. I did not have anything else in the flat but a bed and a kettle. My friend Janine was really supportive, she was able to get me a second-hand cooker whilst Pete helped me by getting me some second-hand sofas and a fridge which helped me out a lot. I was so grateful to them and will never forget their kindness.

I had no visits from my sister when I moved into my flat. It was only when my brother had a nervous breakdown that she felt inclined to visit me late at night and let me know. I made a really good friend called Mary who lived along my balcony. Mary was a lot older than me, she had two older children of her own. I would go around to Mary's at times when I wanted someone to talk to because back then I did not have a mobile phone or even a house phone. We became good friends and she eventually ended up being Godmother to my daughter Leanne. It was hard being a first time mother, especially as I did not have my family support. I did not know where my step-father lived by this time and he was not aware that he even had grandchildren.

My mother or brother did not visit, I do not remember them ever visiting me whilst I lived alone with my daughter. My eldest sister Carole visited maybe once but because she was unwell there was not much she could do to support. I did appreciate her visiting. My sister Joan visited once to show me her new car, but I only ever saw her when I visited her and her family which was often because I enjoyed spending time with my sister and her family, but sadly this was not reciprocated. I found it really hard but quickly realized that I was alone with my daughter so tried to make the most of things.

My friends would visit and that helped with having company, but I was worried that my daughter would not have a family and I did not feel I was enough. It was at this point I started to think about James and convinced myself that he or his family could possibly provide my daughter with the family love that I believed she needed. I decided to visit him and explain that he was her father, I was unsure how he would respond to this because it had been over a year since I last saw him, and we did not exactly end on good terms. I was nervous because I knew he was a violent unstable person, but I thought maybe he would be different with a child. Looking back now I realize I was familiar with violence and being scared, so inviting that back into my life, if I was thinking clearly, I would have kept away in order to protect my daughter. When I went to see him at his mother's home, he was all too happy to be in my daughter's life but stated only if he can be in a relationship with me. This was not what I planned, I also explained to him that I was also raped near the time of conception and I was unsure if she was his child. He still wanted to be with me and help take care of my daughter, he came across as very nice and calm, a bit like when I first met him so I thought I would give it a chance.

Things went very well at first, his family including his parents welcomed me and my daughter, they gave her a lot of attention and love, it all seemed like a great blessing, but I still had reservations. After roughly two months I fell pregnant and the sickness with vomiting came back. I was unable to eat or drink for roughly three months and this made me very weak, I stayed in bed mostly and was unable to even wash myself. James looked after Leanne, he seemed to cope well with this, and he was very good doing the shopping whilst looking after me as well. I appreciated his commitment to this but I knew he wanted me to have the baby which is why he was doing a lot, if he did not help me I probably would have had an abortion which would have made my need for his presence weaker.

His mother and father and other family members were supportive, I had never had so much support before. None of my family visited me or offered to help during this time which was not surprising. I thought my sister who supported me with my daughter would have at least offered some support, but she did not. My mother heard his family were very supportive and I suppose she felt guilty because not long after she offered to buy me a cooker, I had the old cooker for over a year and not sure how she even knew I needed a cooker. However, at the time I was appreciative of her purchasing a cooker for me, one that was safe. I spent most of my pregnancy in bed but started to get up and about at roughly five months. I gave birth to Nathan in the summer of 1990, he was beautiful and really cute, and he weighed the same as his big sister Leanne when she was born at 6lb 4oz. I was relieved and happy. However, my body had to start repairing itself from the distress and lack of nourishment I went through during pregnancy.

It was a big change going from one child to two, but I enjoyed this. I stayed with James and he and his family helped me. My mother and my brother Hudson came to see me at home after I had my son, this was the first time they had paid any attention to me and my first visit by them since I moved into my flat two years prior. Once I started to feel stronger, I wanted to go back to education and get a qualification. I thought I would get support from James because he seemed supportive, but this was not the case… During this part of my journey I started to realize I have potential and wanted to explore this a little further.

Appearance of Nodes

This chapter explores what was like nodes within my life journey. When Nathan was six months I arranged for his and Leanne's christening. It seemed the best thing to do especially as James' mother was a caterer and said she would organize it all. His mother was always nice to me, she had a kind smile and never gave me a 'bad face' even when her son and I went through our many difficulties. I was delighted she would organize things and agreed to the plan. On the morning of the christening my family said they did not want to attend because they felt it was too far and felt his mother was taking over. However, none of them offered to help with the christening and so I was disappointed that they did not want to attend to support me. I pleaded with them to attend and almost had to sell it to them saying that my brother Hudson could be godfather to my son. Eventually they agreed to attend but it was clear they were reluctant.

James and I continued to have problems following the event mostly due to me wanting to go back to education and work. I asked him to leave on numerous occasions and this is when he became aggressive and threatening once again. This behaviour reminded me of his first violent outburst when I was pregnant so I decided that I could never settle down with someone like him and did not trust him. Things did get a little better with James, but he showed aggression and violence if I ever said I wanted space or needed him to leave, I decided to leave my home for the first time and live in a refuge for women fleeing domestic violence.

This was hard because I took my children away from their home environment, but we were safe for a while and that was the main thing. I moved to another borough for a while but eventually went back home, this was because it was a lot harder than I thought it would be. During this time my sister Joan claimed she too was going through domestic violence. I only found out when I visited her home and was told by my mother that she was not there because she had moved to a refuge with her children. I was shocked by this because I had shared all of what I had gone through with her and she had not shared anything with me. I did not even know where she was. This was quite strange especially as I had stayed at her home on numerous occasions and never witnessed any domestic violence or even heated arguments between her and her partner.

Eventually I found out she was staying at a refuge in the other side of London. I visited her often with my children, she claimed she experienced violence and needed to escape. I was very sorry to hear this but was also very suspicious… However, I loved and cared about my sister a lot and looked up to her so believed what she said. I looked after her children for the first summer holidays so that she could have some space because I knew what it was like living in a refuge. At this point James was around and did help with the children, I also had his nieces and nephew visit so that they could all play together. James did not like my sister much as he felt that I looked up to her and did not believe her to be worthy of this. I always ignored him because she was my sister. However, whilst my nieces was staying with me, one of them had been telling James things that I had been saying about him. James was all too happy to let me know this.

I was shocked to hear this and confronted her. She was about 10 or 11 years old at the time. However, Natalie did not have anything to say or even show remorse so because I saw her as a child and knew things were difficult for them at that time. I did not make a big thing about it but told her she should not do this again. Upon reflection I now realize my sister Joan must have been talking about me to her daughter and there was clearly no family loyalty. James said he felt I had the right to know, although he was right, I do think he did get some pleasure out of telling me because he did not think my sister and her family were supportive enough to me. Although he was not right for me, he made a fair point with his views about my sister and her family.

Eventually I had to leave my flat for good when James tried to strangle me. He was arrested, and I was waiting at my mother's house for them to give me a place at another refuge. During this time my sister had moved on from the refuge she had lived in and was living in a hotel. Joan offered me her friends flat that was not too far away from her. Her friend was also fleeing domestic violence and had to leave her flat. My mother advised me not to live there as it was not safe, so I refused the offer. I eventually got allocated a place at the refuge that my sister had lived in, this was good news because my children were familiar with the place and it was close to my sister. I contacted my sister with excitement and told her the good news, although she did not sound too happy about it. When I arrived at the refuge at about 11pm with all my belongings they said I could not stay there because my sister had been there and told them not to take me in. I am not sure what she told them, but I was devastated.

They eventually found me another bed somewhere else, me and my children did not arrive there until roughly 2 o'clock in the morning. I did not speak to my sister for about two weeks but eventually contacted her and asked her why she told the refuge not to take me, she gave a very weak reply saying she did not want her partner to find her through me. This made no sense because she wanted me to live in her friend's flat that was closer to where she was, so I know that was not the real reason... This was probably the beginning of me realising the type of sister I could possibly have but sadly remained in denial for many years following this incident.

I eventually settled temporarily in a women's refuge where I started to take my daughter Leanne to school and took my son Nathan to part-time Nursery. I also started a short course at an adult community centre that was at the end of the road. I felt free and refreshed and stayed there for several months whilst they sorted out me being accepted within the borough. The refuge had three stages, I was accepted at the final stage and was due to move there in a few weeks when James' sister was moved into the refuge in a room adjacent to mine. I was shocked and horrified to see her as I was not aware that she had experienced any kind of difficulties. We spoke and I asked her not to tell James. Although she promised not to say anything, I did not trust her so asked the refuge to move me ASAP and not let her know where I was going. I went to the final stage and was there for some time. I heard his sister had moved out of the refuge and only stayed there for a week. I was suspicious and had a bad feeling she would tell her brother.

I was right… One day when I picked up my daughter from school and was making my way back to the refuge James pulled up in a vehicle alongside the road and attacked me with Nathan in my arms. My daughter was running away and I rushed to keep her from going in the road whilst protecting myself and my son. I managed to get back to the refuge and called the police. The refuge management felt the safety of the women and myself had been compromised and as a result I had to move out. I still can't believe I was thrown out like an old shoe… They found me a hostel not too far so I could still take my children to school and nursery but there was no safety net or support.

There was an office where you could use the telephone if need be in the daytime but at night there was no one. I felt vulnerable and alone but knew I had to make the best of a bad situation. I spent many hours sorting out my housing situation, I no longer had the support of the refuge.

I wrote to the local MP and councillors for the borough ward where I was staying and to my surprise they kindly responded and agreed to give me support. Along with the local politician and my perseverance I was eventually offered decent accommodation, a beautiful three bedroom house in the town Centre, it was perfect... I received this offer December 1993 and moved in January 1994. Little did I know, this would be my first real home and that I would live there for the next twenty four years of me and my children's lives and the first ten years would be like the appearance of nodes with my first home resembling the part of a plant stem from which one or more leaves emerge.

Clearing Of The
Withered Weeds

Luke 6:44

This chapter will explore the people, situations and things that needed to move in order for me to transition to the next stage of my life. When I received the keys for my new home, I was very excited and quickly started to move in. James was around and on his best behaviour. However, I knew he had not changed so when I told him I would never live with him again and he became angry and started to behave in threatening way, I was ready. I recall walking calmly to my front door and opened it and told him to get out. I could tell he was shocked, but he knew he no longer had power over me, so he left. He was holding a bottle of drink that he brought with him but when he was outside, he saw my living room window was open and so poured the bottle all over my new sofas. I was not surprised but also knew he was petty, it was over. I could never welcome him back in my home, it would be too risky. I also had other weeds to clear. Although I still cared deeply for my sister Joan, I realized I was making most of the effort. I stopped going to her house on a weekly basis and this soon became monthly and then yearly, we eventually became very distant.

For each tree is known by its own fruit. For men do not gather figs from thorns, nor do they pick grapes from a bier bush.

I was now entering a new stage in my life and looked forward to what this might be.

Emerging Stems

I settled very quickly into my new home, I got to know my neighbours who were friendly, and the surrounding area was nice too. I was aware there was a church at the end of my road because I had asked the vicar to bless my home before I moved in. His name was Father Geoff, I decided I would go along to the church the following Sunday because I always wanted my children to go to a church based school. This worked well as they did have a school attached to the church, although it was a few miles away it was not too far. Father Geoff said he would put in a good word for me and a place was opened for my daughter. My son was younger but he also had a place and so he attended the nursery pre-school half day. This was a great blessing to find a good school in such a short time and I was appreciative of this. However, my main reason for attending church was to get my children in the school, which I accomplished. My plan was not to go back to the church, but God had other plans. Now that the children were in school, I had some free time. There was a nice elderly lady who was very friendly and supportive. I had a huge back garden and she arranged for the caretaker of the church to clean and clear my garden. I was grateful for this as it was something that needed doing along with all the other odd jobs. A whole new world of support and friendship was opening up, I was grateful, and I showed this by attending church now and again. I started to volunteer to run the crèche at the annual church bazaar and this became a regular annual theme which led to helping out now and again with Sunday school.

When my son started full time in reception, I decided to look for work. I applied for a job working therapeutically with children and babies in a family Centre. The church was one of my references and I was successful with obtaining the job which was part-time and only a twenty minute walk from my children's school. Perfect... I was so excited. Good things seem to be happening one after the other. It was not long after this I heard James had been sentenced to three years in prison for a drug related crime. I felt a dark cloud removed from me, I felt a sense of freedom and justice but did not realize there would be more good things to come.

My job was specifically to work with children and deliver parenting programmes but my role was so much more than this. Assisting parents and carers to develop positive attachments to their children and babies was an enjoyable experience and it did not really feel like a job at all. I found my creative talents very quickly and before long I was in charge of developing focus themed play in and outside the Centre which involved organizing opportunities for free holidays for low income families that attended the Centre, this included accompanying the families on holiday to support them, I also brought along my own children. I think this helped with not only role modelling but to show the parents and children that although I was staff as no other staff wanted to attend, I was also able to share their experiences and have a good time. I believe this actually helped us to bond because following the holiday, parents mostly came to me for advice or just to have a chat. This caused a little bit of tension between the Full time play facilitator and I. However, I did not let this interfere with my role in the Centre. I actually liked the full-time worker because she had great sense of humour and made me laugh but she did have little bit of a callous streak.

Fortunately, I had a good relationship with the manager who hired me, she informed me that the Full-time worker did not like me very much and so she did not tell her I had a criminal conviction on my check as believed she would have made problems for me. I was of course very grateful to Jocelyn she was a very nice lady and she was fair. Because I was so grateful I would go above and beyond my role and assist with anything that helped the families or helped make the Centre run smoother. One Christmas a charity donated many presents to the children, I travelled to central London to collect them and then sat and ended up wrapping about 25 presents. I only planned to wrap about four or five but ended up doing the lot. I really loved doing things for the families and would always go above and beyond to help and ensured I was never judgmental to their situation. I remember a few parents thanking me for my authenticity and kindness. I could relate to these families, my own childhood was difficult, I do believe if my family had the opportunity to attend a family Centre with a supportive environment maybe things would have been different. I believe this thought helped motivate me to be what I would have wanted to see and have for my own experience growing up. This also helped me to be more attentive to my own children as this same thought of doing things differently was extended to them. I would organize weekly activities for them that involved dancing, football, cinema or going to soft play areas for them to let off steam. I ensured they had nice furniture for their rooms with what I could afford and would have monthly dining outs. I claimed compensation just after my 18th birthday for my eye injury and although it took roughly four years I finally got a pay-out of a few thousand pounds. I was delighted and decided to take my children on a family holiday. I did offer to pay for my mother to attend with us but she declined at the time.

It was the summer of 1997 and we were all ready to go on a two week break. I was really excited when we arrived at our beautiful sunny destination because my grandmother (my mother's mother) came to spend some time with us at the hotel, my uncle dropped her off. It was challenging because my grandmother was recovering from a stroke and so needed care. Looking after her, washing her clothes and looking after my children was a lot but I enjoyed this special time, we went to the beach, had breakfast, lunch and dinner together whilst having many laughs and jokes along the way.

Meeting my grandmother and spending the time with her was precious as this was the first and the last time I would see her. She died several years later. I enjoyed travelling with my children so much I arranged with the rest of the money to organize another holiday to Florida. Yes Florida, I think I was more excited than them. We spent three weeks in Orlando over the Christmas of 1998. We visited over five theme parks, Walt Disney World, Epcot, MGM Studios, Animal Kingdom, Water World, Sea World, Universal Studios and Magic Kingdom. We went to different excursions and even went into the community to a place called Jacksonville Westwood. Myself and the children went along to a Centre where they welcomed us. My son took part in the basketball tournament and won a medal. I also helped teach the Centre netball. We all got on so well they offered me a job with accommodation. I appreciated their offer but was unable to take it up because it would mean leaving everything I know to live out there with my children and I was not prepared to take that risk but it was a great offer and I will never forget their kindness. In 1999 things changed. It was in May, my mother had been worried because she had not been able to get hold of my brother. I knew at this point something was not right. My brother Hudson had passed away in his flat, they called it sudden death syndrome. One evening when I got in from work, my sister Joan called me on the phone sounding very desperate, she told me at this point that the police and landlord managed to get into Hudson's flat and found that he had passed away. I broke down in tears immediately. It was so inappropriate for Joan to tell me this by telephone as she also lived in London but there was not much I could do, she was never very mindful. I was devastated, it was such a shock to the system, and I could not believe he was gone. My brother suffered with mental illness similar to my sister Carole and my mother. Although, he tried really hard to cope with his illness and live the best life he could. I loved my brother a lot, we were not very close due to his illness, mostly because we lived quite far from each other and I was busy looking after my family. He did visit me about six months before he died, this was the first time he visited me by himself.

I appreciated him making the effort, we had a nice chat and the visit was enjoyable but now he was gone, it felt like he was gone too soon and did not have a chance to live out his life. However, I do believe he went to a better place because I could see he was not happy, I don't think he fully came to terms with his illness although he never talked about his feelings to me. My brother Hudson was a gentle and good person with a great sense of a humour but the smiles and the laughs became fewer as time went on. Once, when I was approaching my teens, my mother instructed him to 'beat' me, I cannot remember exactly why, I suppose she had many reasons but I do recall being very scared because I knew what Lion was like. It was common back then for older siblings to discipline younger siblings. I ran away quickly out of fear, my brother who was a lot bigger, chased after me. When I could not run anymore I knelt, cowering in a corner. I was petrified but when he got to me, he only pretended to hit me, I did not feel any blows, nothing like I expected from someone who had the potential to do some serious damage. I was surprised and a little confused but mostly relieved. I think my mother knew, because she never asked him to do that again. Hudson proved he was not like his father. Although he wanted to have a good relationship with Lion but that never happened. Lion often criticized him and never gave any encouragement. He beat him a lot as a child and there were some whisperings that he may have sexually abused him too.

I miss Hudson but believe he is in a better peaceful place. Soon after my brother's death I started to get dreams that involved a man that I did not know. It was a dream that also involved my mother but she looked very young and slim in the dream.

I told my mother about the dream and asked her about the man, I said he seemed to know me in the dream but I did not know him. My mother went quiet during the phone call and a few days later she told me she needed to speak with me and would be visiting. I am not sure why but I was not surprised and had a good idea at what she was going to say. When she came to my home she explained that Lion was not my real father and that she had an affair during her marriage to him because she was so unhappy with his violence. I was understanding because I know what she went through with Lion. This was the first time my mother was vulnerable and honest with me but it did not take long for her to snap back into her old ways where she did not want to speak about it and refused to open up about Lion. After telling me such a secret she wanted me to continue to keep it a secret, I realized she only told me to release herself of guilt and had no intentions of supporting me through this. The year seemed to get worse before it could get better. James was released from prison and wanted to have access to the children. I refused so he went through the family courts. I was not comfortable with this as I did not believe that his motives for accessing the children was because he cared about them. I believe it was to be annoying to me but I worked as instructed with the Courts. He did get access every 2 weeks, I stated I wanted him to pick up the children from school on the weekends that he would have them and drop them off at school for the Monday so that he had no reason to come to my house.

This was very hard for me because this was the person that threatened my life and attacked me on several occasions in front of the children. He was also just coming out of prison so when the courts allowed him access I felt betrayed and let down by a system that was supposed to be there to protect women like myself and their children.

To be honest I was surprised at this outcome but was also very angry at the family court welfare officer that completed the report for the court because I felt she did not listen to my concerns relating to the welfare of my children but was more working from the red tape stand point of father's entitlement to spend time with their children. I also believe that because I never went to court and had James charged for his previous violence, this went against me so would advise anyone who has been subjected to violence to take the perpetrator to

COURT. Even if you go to a safe place or the abuser seems nicer, never trust it... Going to court means they are then charged and therefore you have evidence of what has happened to you, I did not have any evidence apart from my word which clearly did not amount to much. My children were never happy to attend every other weekend and when I tried to address some of the issues with James he refused to listen or compromise. I knew this was the reason he wanted the children, to be mean and also have some access to my life through them, he also moved down the road to me to be even more annoying and intimidating. I realized this situation could work for me or against me. I could spend the next several years arguing and going back and forth or make positive changes. I spoke to the children about their time with him and explained that if ever they were there and felt uncomfortable or wanted to leave then they should come straight home. They were scared of James so they said they wanted to continue to go.

Petals

I decided I wanted to make some serious changes in my life especially since finding out about Lion. I didn't discuss this with him for a number of years for sixteen years to be exact, I am not sure how I kept quiet but guess I did for my mother... Over these years I accepted my mother would not support me with this but also aware that she has mental health issues that I think interfered with her mind set and ability to be the mother I needed her to be. Although she was very good at showing compassion and support to others, mostly strangers so unsure how much of her behaviour was related to illness, character, or both.

I decided that it was important for me to tell Lion myself. My mother did not do this for me or for herself so it was down to me, it was so hard but worth it. I eventually spoke to Lion about it following the death of my eldest sister and he agreed to have a paternity test which was the confirmation I needed to help me to eventually have clarity. At the time, he said he did not want to know the outcome of the test but I think deep down he knew the truth and there was nothing he could do about it. This was my second feeling of liberation with confirmation. I was familiar with being dismissed and neglected that I would fall into that role of not acknowledging my own feelings as a person. However, there was a positive to this information and that was the man that was so violent and who had also molested me as a small child was not my real father. This was a relief... Most people would be upset to hear such news but I felt liberated. Not that it excused what he done, far from it...

He is still accountable but knowing his blood did not run through me or my children helped me to have a sense of separation from what he did to me. This happened over the years but it also motivated me to think that I could possibly, one day have a relationship with my biological father. This shifted a lot of negative feelings inside of me that was connected to my earlier abuse and it allowed me to start to feel a little more confident and helped me on my journey to explore my identity through establishing a faith. My journey also enabled me to understand that although I do have a biological father I do not know, I also have a heavenly father who I do know and who knows me. I would actually prefer not to know my biological father, especially if he knew about me and did not make any effort. Also, I do ask myself what type of man has an affair with a married woman... Maybe he would not be the decent man I imagine him to be if he knew and was still prepared to go ahead with the affair, so it could be a matter of 'what you don't know, don't hurt'.

I started to attend church regularly and felt this was a positive consistent thing in my life. I also went to see a careers officer at the time because I wanted to become a family court welfare officer. I had a great passion for working with children and families, from my experience there was not enough diversity in the family courts system, most if not all were white middle class who had little knowledge of culture or raising working class families. I was told I had to become a Probation Officer first so at this point my career journey began..

My first application to the Probation service was exciting because I passed the first stage and attended the assessment centre. I remember this was really difficult, there were a number of different verbal reasoning tests, an exam, role play and a video analysis. Unfortunately I did not pass this stage but I attended the feedback session and was advised to get more experience. I had not long completed my HNC in Early Childhood course so at this point I applied to Open University and completed a Social Science qualification. Following this I applied to Probation again. I then got to the assessment stage for the second time.

To cut a long story short, I actually applied about three times before I was accepted, each time I attended for feedback and I went away to improve myself for the next application. For my last unsuccessful application, I volunteered to be a mentor to young people at risk of crime. I found this constructive, rewarding and enjoyable. I completed a 6 month training course and then attended an away on an activity weekend with other potential mentors where we participated in a number of different team building activities with the potential mentees. This was really good. I was not just able to overcome my fear of heights and built up a good rapport with the young people but also became a mentor to a young female at risk of offending. On the coach journey back from the weekend away, the organizers asked all mentees to choose who they would like as a mentor and I was chosen by a young female. I found this extremely motivating and a privilege that I was chosen. Mentoring was rewarding and another great way for me to give back to society. This experience helped me immensely with following the applications to the Probation service. I was finally accepted. This was a great achievement for me.

Not just because my determination and persistent paid off but rather due to the previous kindness and support I received from my own probation officer and how important it was for me to use this opportunity to contribute to positive change in peoples' lives just as he did mine. My journey with the London Probation Service was both exciting and challenging at the same time. It was exciting because to be accepted in this trainee role far exceeded my expectation for my life, I knew at that point that I would work hard to complete the training.

There were numerous tasks such as attending University to complete a degree, training to deliver accredited group programs, a diploma in Probation Studies and a national vocational qualification level 4. I also completed an evidence based folder of my practical work whilst holding and supervising a small case load of low risk offenders. I had to train within the courts and visit prisons. There was a vast amount of work to do but I sailed through all of it and even completed my training earlier than the expected date. There were certainly frustrating times but I did not let this discourage me it actually made me more determined. I found this journey helped me to realize just how practical and focused I really was.

The day I graduated was one of the proudest days of my life. To put on my robe and hat and hear my name being called to collect my degree is a day I will never forget. I invited my mother and Lion to this day, my mother said she did not want to attend at the last minute, with no real reason why but I managed to encourage her to attend as I would not have felt comfortable with just Lion and me in attendance.

Following becoming a qualified Probation Officer I was placed at a London office. My case load increased quickly and I was managing high risk cases, attending MAPPA meetings, child protection meetings and court duty. I really enjoyed the role, I had a supportive manager and great colleagues who always made being at work enjoyable despite how hard our job was. Although the work was tough we could all have a laugh and we also got on very well. I felt a great sense of achievement and was motivated to do the role. I started to reflect on my life and how far I came and realized this could only be God and knew I wanted to explore this further.

During my time at the new office I made a few good friends, one of which I did my training with as we were both placed at the same office, her name was Ruthie. Ruthie was much younger than me but very mature, she had recently married a young man and both was devout Christians. Ruthie was what I would call a modern day Christian, she often spoke about her faith but in a relatable way, she always arrived early for work and seemed to manage her case load effortlessly. Ruthie had great faith and seemed to also have an evangelistic approach as more and more people would also openly discuss their faith and invite each other to church. I remember thinking to myself one day, I want to know her God.

I also recall, training with a man who was a Christian in my group and again I was interested in his faith which was Seven Day Adventist (like my grandmother). I believe my journey with the probation service was not just about the work and qualifying as an officer but also to be exposed to Godly people who were relatable and nothing like the people in the extreme environment that I was brought up in.

My mother had so many rules and unnecessary behaviours, not to mention the judgmental views. I did not believe God would ever accept me as I am because of this confusing outlook. This changed as I got to know people like Ruthie and others that helped me make the decision to give my life to Christ. This was not an easy decision because I knew I could not turn back once it was done so I needed to be absolutely sure. What sealed the deal for me was the fact that I had achieved goals in life much higher than my own self expectations, I had a great job, my health, nice home and healthy good children.

I knew this could only be God's work and not my own, of course I put in the hard work to build this but I could not have achieved any of it without something more supernatural, the help of God. The gratitude I felt touched me spiritually and mentally and with the help of the church I was attending, I made the arrangements to be baptized into the Anglican faith and then to follow this with my confirmation at the neighbouring Cathedral. This was a very important time in my life, I knew I wanted to be committed to my faith but I was unsure what that journey would be like or what it would look like. I had a lot of disappointments in my relationships and trusting others was hard. At the time I knew this was something I would work on in my relationship with God, could I trust God with my life? Following my confirmation I continued to attend church weekly and got involved in church activities as well as becoming a Parochial Church Council member, in addition also a PCC governor for the primary school which meant I met regularly with church members. I enjoyed these roles as it gave me a sense of belonging and helped me build my confidence.

I also enjoyed my role as a Probation Officer and was managing my high case load well. I even attended work at the weekend where I delivered accredited group programmes.

However, I decided I would explore some other roles, mainly because I had grown but there were also some changes happening in Probation that meant the teams were to change. I decided to apply for a Senior Practitioner role within the Youth Offending Team (YOT). I did not even expect to get an interview for the job but I was blessed enough to not just get an interview but to also get the job. At the time I thought, what a great opportunity. Because I did not expect it I was not really fully prepared to move into a new job especially one that gave me management responsibilities.

Can I really do this, I thought to myself...

I decided to take the opportunity and the more I thought about it the more excited I became. I started in my new role as Senior Practitioner following my notice period with the Probation Service, my management duties were overseeing four Officers and one Education Officer. Managing 5 staff members was a huge challenge for me but I was confident I could do it, mainly because I am a people person but I also had a great passion and commitment for the work. The role involved attending numerous management meetings, supervision, and writing reports. I also had a small case load at times. Although I enjoyed the role, the staff worked really hard so did not need to be micro managed. However, there was one member of staff that I had to be firm with in terms of some behaviours he was allowed to get away with in the past, they were not acceptable. Some people stated he did not like being managed by a woman. He had been there for the longest so was complacent in doing what he wanted to do so I had to address this with him. There were challenges in this role but it gave me a great introduction to management experience. It also gave me a sense of confidence because I was able to overcome the challenges but also achieve some great outcomes.

This included improved protocols for staff, appropriate allocation of cases whilst building and maintaining partnerships but mainly I was able to implement positive workshops to motivate and educate the young clients. I did this for roughly 4 years before I decided to explore another role. I applied for a service manager position, it was good money and when I checked the job specification I believed I had the skills and the knowledge to do the job. Although I was confident, I was sure there would be huge competition so did not expect to get shortlisted. Fortunately, I was called for an interview but when I arrived it was not for the role I applied for.

The interview panel explained to me that with my wealth of experience and knowledge they would like to put me forward for another Service Manager role, it was the same salary so I decided to go with the flow even though I had no idea what the role would entail... They explained that I would have to deliver a presentation and would give me 20 minutes to prepare. So here I was, completely out of my depth but had a gut feeling this would be something exciting. Over the years I have noticed that I have strengths in delivering presentations and I like the challenge of doing things spontaneously. At this point I knew I would rise to the challenge. I did... The panel was amazed at how quickly I not only got my head around the theme of the presentation but also how confidently I delivered it. The role was in line with my skills and was a much better role than the one I applied for. However, it was hugely challenging. I was successful in getting the job but had to dive straight in which meant there was much firefighting.

I managed a service of thirty staff and directly line managed four team leaders but that went down to three after six months. I also oversaw roughly 134 clients across six London boroughs and fifteen landlords, it was completely over whelming for me but I loved it. I enjoyed that I could use my creative skills but also done a lot of travelling. I had my own laptop and mobile phone and eventually even had my own office for a while. This was a great role, I was a service manager for services such as ex- offenders coming out of prison, those with dependency and substance misuse issues, those with mental health issues, rough sleepers and young people across six London boroughs with a total of 23 properties across these areas.

I had a huge role. My role had previously been done by 2 people, I guess to save money they decided to only have one person fill the role which meant I had to constantly fire fight and complete exit strategies for a Council who was not happy with the services I inherited. Although I tried to repair and bridge relationships, it was too late for some, a few services had to be decanted and handed back. However, I did have a small service left in one of the boroughs that I was determined to save which I did. There was a lot of work and a lot of pressure but the role allowed me to be creative and showcase my skills in ways I was never able to in my past roles.

I was nervous but also very excited about my new role so decided to invest in myself and do a course that would help me deliver my role in management more effectively. I applied for a Master's degree with a London University to do Social Enterprise, especially as this was where my organisation was going according to their vision statement.

Unfortunately, the course did not have enough applicants so was not being delivered for that year I applied. I was disappointed at this because the course content looked so interesting but did not want to give up as I really wanted to do something. I explored the courses on offer and decided to apply for Coaching Psychology, I felt this would help me improve my management skills with staff. I was successful with my application, it was a Master's which included two research modules. Although, it meant balancing work, family and study at a high level, I was up for the challenge. I did ask my employers if they were willing to sponsor me but they refused, I did not let them know I would still do the course because it did not affect my working hours as my lecture dates were all on the weekends.

Within work, I was innovative and managed to re-birth a new name for the service by organising a survey to staff to pick out of 3 names they would like to be called, following this a celebrated event was also arranged where staff and residents were invited and the local councillor attended as a

VIP guest, where he pulled the name out of the hat. Amongst my achievements was to build up the reputation for the organisation. There had been some bad press which resulted in sponsors and contract holders wanting to withdraw support. I spent a lot of my time building and repairing relationships that thankfully resulted in the organisation securing a new contract. This was a great achievement for me, my team and the organisation. This did not just bring new job opportunities but it also improved the charities reputation. However, the rumour surrounding mismanagement of funds continued to grow... The charity was accused several months before I started in role of alleged fraud within their finances.

As a result, this led to a distrust from funders and key stakeholders which caused a decline in income that unfortunately affected all departments including mine. I was asked to organise and deliver a re-structure within my service. I tried to deliver this in a transparent way by visiting individual schemes, explain what was going on and asked them for feedback on what they would like the service to look like, there were a few options that I had managed to create that would work but meant staff had to re-apply for their positions.

I was not happy that this had to happen but the powers that be made the decision, fortunately I managed to protect the Team leaders so they were able to assist with the recruitment process. The roles were both externally and internally advertised so I had a huge amount to arrange and put all this together including adverts and conduct interviews. Most staff did secure their jobs but not all 27 staff were successful. This was not all bad as we did manage to recruit some new staff that was much needed if we would have a fresh start.

I learnt so much from this process but it was probably one of the most stressful times in my life because not only did I have this huge role and huge change within my team but my mother had a stroke in the middle of this. I did take some time out of work whilst my mother spent three months in hospital following her stroke. I spent much of my time at the hospital and remember feeling very scared about what might happen.

The stroke was a very bad one and had affected her right side, apparently this is not meant to be as bad as the left side but it was still really worrying. I prayed for God to keep her alive and he did, the hospital done a great job with her rehabilitation and I was so grateful for everything.

When my mother was finally allowed home, along with the discharge team we put together a great package tailored to mum's needs which included a lot of practical support. This worked for a while but had a few teething problems like most things that are new for people to adjust to. Mum was very different to how she used to be. My mother lived a life like a spitfire. Very strong in her personality as described in previous chapters and almost extreme in her views and even in her actions at times, with a stern approach.

Following her stroke she presented very different, not sure if this was because the stroke scared her as much as it did us. The other idea was it could have been something that happened chemically in her brain that caused her to change, I think it was probably a mixture of both.

My mother became very quiet and appeared softer but seemed to also have an improved sense of humour. I spent much of my time balancing my job, home life and caring for her. Mum was fortunate enough to have adaptions in the home, a commode upstairs and downstairs, meals on wheels and carers attending on a daily basis. Between managing mum's care, my family, work and study it became very difficult to manage it all effectively. I became very low in energy and realised that I would have to make a sacrifice. I arranged a meeting with my Supervisor at the university and explained my situation, both my supervisor and colleagues were very supportive, I decided to complete that year as I had already started but would defer the second year and complete it at a later time.

Although this helped, I still was struggling because mum had been complaining about carers which I felt was just her resistance to change rather than anyone actually not doing their job.

I spent a lot of my time balancing between all my responsibilities. My sisters did help her, especially Carole. Although Carole had her own mental health issues she was able to go to mum's and help with cooking and cleaning. Joan did do some things like make doctors' appointments and take mum to these appointments. However, it was inconsistent... Due to both having their own illnesses it meant on numerous occasions I had to attend or make the necessary arrangements. This was frustrating as I would never really know when I would have to step in as it was mostly random and usually at the inconvenient times. Due to winning a new contract in work I knew there would be great opportunities opening up for my service and also for me, not only did we gain the contract but we also took charge of the existing contract that was in place to deliver this work. This would require me to actually take on more work and possibly also achieve a promotion to a Director position which is the role above Service Manager.

This was a great time career wise for me, it was what I had spent my whole working career trying to achieve, however, it was bitter sweet... Although it was a great opportunity, I knew I was not in a position to move forward with the organisation to this new place. I was tired through caring, working and worried that if my mother did not get the care she needed she might end up having another stroke. I was not about to make this happen so made what was one of the hardest decisions of my career life, and gave up my work to become her full-time carer. My manager gave me an alternative, asking me to either apply for the next role or I could take voluntary redundancy.

I decided the redundant route was the better option for me at that time. I was unsure as to what caring for my mother would look like but the worry for her was a lot stronger that any promotion. I believed that I could always go back to finding work at any time but I only have one mother that I believed at the time needed me and because I had prayed for her to live I believe that God was giving me another opportunity with her and I did not want to miss this important special time. I subsequently went on what they call Garden leave, this is basically staying at home whilst getting paid as Human Resources sort out all the particulars relating to the redundancy package that I was entitled to.

This suited me as I could spend more time with my mother arranging and organising her care. I joined all the carers support organisations and did a lot of research on the type of support needed for people who were recovering from stokes. By the end of spring that year, I eventually received a really good redundancy package that I was pleased with and parted ways with the organisation. Although, several months later I found out that the Charity went into liquidation and then administration. Several months later the charity ceased to exist and they filed for bankruptcy. I knew there had been problems in their finances but was surprised that they took a fall so soon, I thought they had at least another 3 years... I realised at that moment I made the right decision to leave. My transition into being a caregiver took a while, there were a few milestones and challenges, but mostly I had many celebrations of achievements and accomplishments when I became a full-time carer, these were totally unexpected. My life as a carer had been amazing and I experienced beyond anything that I could imagine, I will not include my life as a carer in this book, maybe for my next one.

Although, my journey takes on a new shape, after caring full time for several years I do feel I will always be there for my mother as her daughter who cares deeply. I managed to get to know my mother a lot better through spending so much time with her, although recognising our differences and the occasional disconnection within our fragmented relationship. I also often think about the differences between me and my siblings and come to the idea of the nature nurture debate. I would like to explore this next but want to also share this great scripture from the bible which I resonates this part of my journey.

Where once there were thorns, cypress trees will grow. Where nettles grew, myrtles will sprout up. These events will bring great honour to the LORD's name; they will be an everlasting sign of his power and love."(Isaiah 55:13)

Nature Versus Nurture

Nature versus Nurture is the scientific, cultural, and philosophical debate about whether human culture, behaviour, and personality are caused primarily by nature or nurture. It is believed that nature is responsible for the growth of a person from the fetus level until development into a normal adult. The nature influence suggests a genetic makeup of a human being is responsible for their sex, skin colour, colour of their eyes and hair as well as distinguishing features which are inherited, whilst nurture most commonly refers to the influences of experience and environment.

The nature vs. nurture debate has been analysed and explored through studies by psychologist for decades. During these studies no one has been able to make a distinct decision. Some say nurture has more effect than nature and vice versa. Heredity is the transmission of genetic characters from parents to offspring. It is dependent upon the segregation and recombination of genes during meiosis and fertilization. Jerome Kagan (2010) believes Nature and nurture work together to produce a personality the way humidity and cold come together to generate snow," says Jerome Kagan, Ph.D., author of The Temperamental Thread: How Genes, Culture, Time, and Luck Make Us Who We Are.

My interpretation within this debate is the biological approach which is the focus on genetic hormonal, neurochemical explanations of behaviour. Nature is all about those characteristics that are inherited from genes or from your parents. Behaviourism explains that behaviour is learned from the environment through conditioning. Nurture is about those characteristics which develop from experiences and environment.

I believe my journey laid out in this book has probably been shaped, moulded and directed not just by my heavenly Father but possibly through my biological make-up and my environment. I say this because the opportunities I have had although I have worked hard have been beyond my expectations and the expectations of family members. When I was young my mother would always say I would be a teacher, not sure why, maybe because as a child I was always pretending to teach a class of invisible children, I also believed that I wanted this for a number of years. Although, I began a journey wanting to work with children but this was mostly through the care route rather than the educational route.

I never had any other encouragement, I never had toys or books only what the school or friends provided, however, I do remember a friend of my mother giving me what looked like a beautiful toy telephone that was actually a radio. When I visited her house with my mother I kept playing with it and looking at it, she ended up saying I could have it. I thought this was so kind of her. My school work was never checked or discussed, in fact there was no real place that I could do my homework, I remember doing it on the stairs at home once. I was never asked how I did in tests, my education did not seem at all important to people in my household.

My mother would attend parents evening but it was only because it was mandatory, we never spoke about what teachers had said to her, never discussed me doing better or working harder and there was not any praise for anything I did do well. However, I always enjoyed school, I loved to learn new things and had a good approach to most of my subjects. I would not describe myself as particularly bright, not on paper anyway or according to the education boards standard and would tend to be nearer the bottom in exams than closer to the top, unless it was PE, history or drama, however, by the time I got to senior high school I enjoyed English because I had a really nice teacher. I was not too bad in those subjects and this was without encouragement. I do sometimes wonder what I could have achieved in school with the right amount of encouragement. My view of school was disrupted and tainted following the attack from the geography teacher, and this is probably why I dislike that subject even today. When she physically abused me this also affected me emotionally and mentally. I was not only working through the traumatic injury to my eye and the ongoing treatment and surgeries but now I no longer felt safe in school.

The place that once provided a safety net no longer existed. When I was placed in the new school, I started to play truant, smoke and spent more and more time with 'likeminded friends' which led to my first arrest and other problems. By the time I went to senior high school, I had given up, only going to school when I felt like it and turning up at whatever time. I did not even bother to go back to get my exam results and nobody ever enquired. School no longer served a purpose. I guess feeling safe was more important to me than my education at the time.

Comparing it to my motivation and discipline today to achieve and maintain employment whilst progressing within roles, I realize that my love for learning help me to enjoy studying and achieved not just one Degree but two and a Masters at that. Could it be possible that by nature I am biologically made to be ambitious? Does my drive come from something I am born with?

I would like to explore this within my last chapter. I will be exploring nature versus nurture using an analysis of some literary reviews looking at stories and views of academics whilst implementing a little information on some evidence with statistics and conclude with the benefits or not of nature and nurture relating to my story summary. I included this chapter because I think I have had a very unique experience, I was born in a family with a lot of dysfunction and where abuse occurred on a daily basis. I did not visually experience or observe any love and care between my parents because all they did was fight and argue. I was neglected whilst experiencing physical and sexual abuse and lived most of my childhood in isolation with family members who showed no interest in my wellbeing. I had no one in or out of the family home to speak to but as a teenager, I found a trusted adult in my Probation Officer who listened to me and helped me believe in myself. Although things took a while to get better I found another trusted friend and that was Jesus Christ who has continued to be a very prominent part of my life.

I remember going to see a Christian counsellor and he said he found it hard to believe that someone who had been through the things I had been through could achieve as much as I did. He felt I should not have had the confidence or ambitions that I had which came across as if he thought I was making it up.

I quickly stopped seeing him because he was clearly into labels and stereotypes and had no real idea of the power of God... I thought it was a real shame that even as a Christian he doubted the power of what God can do in people's lives. I know now that it is not about where you start in life it is about where you end up... Some people do not start their life with much but end up achieving. In fact, one can argue that it is mostly those who start off with very little that probably end up working much harder to achieve a lot more for their lives.

Oprah Winfrey spent her childhood struggling with a strange dichotomy: academic achievement and a dysfunctional home life. However, she achieved a career that has spanned from every form of media and beyond. She has had a turn in being an actress, talk show host, producer, and philanthropist.

Among Oprah Winfrey's greatest accomplishments is being Chairwoman and CEO of both Harpo Productions and The Oprah Winfrey Network. What a shame it would have been if she lived her life or limited herself according to where she started. John Rockefeller was the lowly son of a dodgy con artist and high-school student in suburban Cleveland, Ohio.

He failed to attend high school. Rockefeller made his mark in the oil industry, starting Standard Oil and ultimately creating a monopoly on the entire industry. By 1902, Rockefeller was worth $200 million, and before his death he would amass a fortune of more than one billion dollars. I can honestly say that I do not blame anyone for what I went through and do not feel angry towards my family because they had their own brokenness which is what caused them to behave in the way they did. I forgive them but I know that in order to move forward in my own life I have to accept that not all of them will be able to continue with me on my journey. Sadly, some family members still have the destructive behaviours or have sadly passed on.

I am content and no longer feel the need to look for family or the father I never knew but realize I have a Father in heaven who loves me and takes care of my everyday life and will continue to be with me throughout my journey. I do often wonder about why I am so different to not just my siblings but also the parent figures in my life. This has made me struggle with my sense of belonging and identity which has caused difficulties in my personal relationships with others.

I will now analyse a study of triplets who did not grow up with their natural parents and the outcomes in their lives that may have effected them or not related to the biological aspect...

A psychiatrist and psychoanalyst named Dr. Peter B. Neubauer wanted to solve the mystery of nature vs. nurture and decided to use children put up for adoption as guinea pigs for his research. In 1962 three triplets David Kellman, Robert Shafran and Edward Galland were given up individually for adoption to different families. In 1980, 18 years later, they accidently re-united by extraordinary quirk of fate. A prominent child-placement agency for Jewish families, intentionally separated a number of twins and multiple-birth siblings and placed them in homes of different socio-economic levels for the purposes of using the children's lives for research. Neubauer told adoptive parents only that they were doing research on adopted children, not on biological siblings separated at birth. The Louise Wise agency facilitated years of research on Eddy, David, and Bob, by sending researchers on house visits. For more than 15 years, they performed psychological testing and took extensive notes and video recordings of the children. The findings of the research is unknown, since the conclusions were never published, and the notes were apparently kept under seal at Yale University until roughly 2065 according to yaledailynews.com (2018).

It wasn't until the documentary filmmakers' put the pressure on the Yale officials now holding the research to authorise limited access of the psychological files to the studied children who requested access. A number of children have still not been informed they were separated at birth from siblings and studied as a part of the multiple-birth-child research. The three triplets had identical looks, similar ways of talking, and common ideas about how to have fun together. Sadly, they also had similar struggles with mental illness growing up. As children, all three displayed separation anxiety, banging their heads against the bars of their cribs; all three experienced depression at times, and all three made visits to psychiatric hospitals as teenagers.

David was placed in an upper-class family with a doctor as his adoptive father; he experienced a rather reserved home life where his father was often unavailable. On the opposite end of the spectrum, Bob was placed in a working-class home with a grocery-store owner as a father who had a very warm and jovial disposition and later became affectionately called the Yiddish nickname "Bubula" by all three boys. Meanwhile, Eddy was placed in a middle-class family with a dad he often clashed with. When the triplets showed up for their first meeting, they were wearing the same shoes. And they did not know or were not speaking to each other at the time.

They would also wear similar polo shirt, they said, 'that kind of stuff happens all the time, and it was very weird.' Larry Wright who interviewed them for the New Yorker stated 'we drift in the direction our genes push us. But ultimately, nurture can be a counterbalance. Just because we are drifting in one direction doesn't mean were destined to be a priest, or a criminal, or whatever.

But it is frightening how powerful genetics is, like way more powerful than I ever considered' this does indicate that our genetic make-up is very powerful and can have a strong influence on us. Below is the timeline and sibling difference but all at the same starting point, I will then go on to describe this in more detail.

Siblings – Journey Through Timeline

Karen (me)	Born into family with Domestic Violence and other Abuse	Enjoyed school, excelled mostly in Physical Education, English and Drama	Teenage years exciting but got a police record, moved out at 15 years and teenage pregnancy	Adult years, 2 children, moved out of area, gained BA Degree and MSc Degree. Numerous jobs 2 management positions
Carole-Anne	Born into family with Domestic Violence and other Abuse	Excelled in most subject areas, received mostly A. Went on to complete A levels and O levels	Teenage years gained good job as bank teller, mostly listening to music in room, rocking diagnosed with mental health at 19 years	Adult years, diagnosed with Schizophrenia, spent over 20 years in supportive living, passed away at 54 years. RIP
Joan	Born into family with Domestic Violence and other Abuse	Attended Pupil Referral Units, did not achieve well academically	Teenage years left school with no formal qualifications, Police record and teenage pregnancy	Adult years, 3 children, moved out the area, gained access certificate, spent over 30 years on benefits has undiagnosed illnesses
Hudson	Born into family with Domestic Violence and other Abuse	Excelled in most subject areas, received mostly A. Went on to complete A levels and O levels	Teenage Years, gained job with an Insurance Company had a car, spent a lot of time playing sports.	Adult years, diagnosed with schizophrenia at 23 years but managed to live independently, passed away at 34 years. RIP

Siblings – Differences

The journey for me and my siblings above indicates how our lives turned out different. Although we all lived and grew up in the same household, it is possible that our interpretation of our experiences has been very different. My eldest sister Carole-Anne was always praised for her academic achievements in school, she was encouraged through having piano lessons and also played the clarinet, she received straight A's and was a model student, not getting into trouble. Carole was also able to get a good job in a bank but I am unsure how long she kept this for. I just recall my mother arguing with her about giving up, or not being able to keep such a good job. However, at home she rocked constantly to music and very rarely communicated with anyone, even when her friends would call to see her she refused to engage with them, it ended mostly with them leaving and going home. Carol was diagnosed with Paranoid Schizophrenia at roughly the tender age of just 19 years but she was troubled many years before this... Carol spent the rest of her adult years on medication until she passed away.

Hudson was similar to Carol, he presented well behaved in school and was a model student, always achieved an A+. Hudson was very good at sports and received numerous medals, mostly gold and a wide range, from snooker to table tennis, badminton, the list is endless, most displayed in the living room on the mantelpiece. He lived at home until he was roughly 24 years old, he managed to get a job and even had a car but by the time he was roughly 23 years he had a psychotic episode and was sectioned under the mental health process. He tried to get himself back on track by getting his own flat and living independently but he became unwell again and was sectioned a few times. However, he did manage to maintain living independently until he passed away.

Hudson's illness affected him in a similar way to Carol. When they were both unwell they would walk about on the street naked, in Hudson's case he would run. This was obviously unacceptable for the public so subsequently led to them both being detained under the mental health act.

Sadly they both also passed away in the same way from a heart condition. I can never be sure as a family, if we got the right type of support and after care as children this would have made a difference to their fate. However, I do strongly believe if an intervention was put in place to protect my eldest sister from my step-father when she first spoke about his abuse when she was just a little girl (roughly 6 years) maybe she could have had an opportunity to be healed through counselling or even by going into foster care where she could have been a lot safer. Through listening to conversations over the years (because I was not born), it is believed that Carole had told a teacher about her abuse and this led to a court case where she had to give a testimony but my mother, unfortunately told the court she was lying, to protect Lion. Subsequently he was not convicted I heard when my step-father returned back to the house after the court case she was subjected to more violence and sexual abuse, she must have felt so betrayed and let down, not to mention frightened and scared when he was let off. By the time he eventually left the house Carole was roughly 16 years old, but it was too late the damage had been done, she had spent sixteen years of her life being molested and beaten, she was never to be the same again.

My step-father was a damaged, sick person who I believe had Jekyll and Hyde personality disorder, he was repeatedly sexually and physically abusive to us as children with my sister Carole as his main target, although she never stated this I would not be surprised if on occasions, he raped my mother too. I also believe that Hudson may have also experienced some form of sexual abuse. I do not think Lion had a gender preference for his sexual abuse, my mother once shared she was sure she caught him in a sexual act with a male friend of the family so I assume he was probably bisexual but of course would never admit it.

I have to believe if Lion was not let back into the house following Carol's testimony in court and our mother got support with her mental health our lives would have turned out very different...

Hudson managed to stay in work for a number of years until he became too unwell to continue. Hudson and Carol were very similar in their life journey as mentioned, although very different in character. Carol was more flamboyant whilst Hudson was quieter in personality but both liked to be perfectionists and neither one had any recognized meaningful relationships. Joan's journey was a little different, she did not do well in school and was seen as the 'dunce one'. Not a very nice term which was used regularly by my stepfather. We were all made to read sections of the newspaper as children, I read well from an early age so was able to keep up with the others. However, Joan did not read well and struggled with this type of exposure, Lion wasted no time in calling her names and belittling her, everyone would always laugh. Lion and my mother still talk about her in this way today.

Joan had her first baby by the time she was 17 years old, she stayed living at home up until she was about 20 years old. Never had a relationship with her first child's father but did spend several years with her last 2 children's father, at this point she learnt to drive and got a car, she even secured a job at the local Town hall for a short period. However, her youngest daughter had several injuries, visited hospital with a broken leg and also a broken arm on 2 separate occasions. It was at this point Joan disclosed she was going through domestic violence, she was found a new place to live very far away and is still in the same area today. Whilst in the new area she became aware of applications to University and how this included a grant and fees to assist with study.

Joan done really well with her applications and even managed to get an access certificate to help with this. However, during the first year of university she became unwell with an undiagnosed illness and then had to drop out… Joan ended up applying to university over 6 times that I am aware of, there could have been more. I became very upset with her one year as she used my name as a reference for her applications and I was contacted by loan companies wanting to know her whereabouts. It became clear that her motivation was not to study but to use this as an income. Although, Joan has not had a job so as far as I know has not formally been in employment since 1980s and has remained on benefits. Although on paper her life journey looks very different, upon reflection it is not that different from Hudson and Carol. It later transpired that it was Joan who allegedly physically abused her youngest daughter and caused her injury of a broken arm and leg through beating, she was never convicted or suffered any consequence for her actions… Sound familiar…?

My journey is pretty much explained throughout the book. However, I should add some distinctive differences. I spent all of my childhood being pushed out to the edges of the family circle, so much that I sought solace in school, school projects and with friends that I was blessed enough to make and sustain. One thing with children is that they are a lot more accepting and adaptable to making and maintaining friendships than adults. This was my main source for what I can describe as acceptance and in some ways also where I probably tried to understand life and a sense of belonging.

I understand now that it was due to my own family's individual brokenness and the damage caused by the abusive environment that caused such dysfunction. By the time I was approaching teenage years, like most girls I was interested in boys and they seemed to be interested in me too. This was a relief, although I was very shy when it came to the opposite sex which is not a surprise but was also a little promiscuous.

This led to a teenage pregnancy. Neil and I were sexually active following the first year of us getting to know each other. I did not have a great perception of myself and certainly struggled with knowing my worth. Neil was a bit of a 'dog in heat' and seemed a lot more experienced with sex than I was but whenever he strayed he would always come back to me so I suppose this gave me a sense of consistency. This was also the first intimacy for me that was not abuse. However, my shyness to boys also made me a little reserved especially to the boys I liked. In general, I would describe myself as having a very determined and persistent character.

I always knew what I wanted and always found a way to get it. This involved attending Girl's Brigade, being in the school play every year, attending the school disco and going to the cinema. All of these were normal things for a child to desire and want to be part of but my mother restricted all access. Thank God I rebelled against these restrictions. I learnt from an early age that if I wanted to do anything enjoyable I would have to do it without my mother's knowledge, and due to the neglect, this was easy to do. This type of attitude pretty much stayed with me all of my life. I did not always make the right decisions and there were consequences for this.

I always wanted to do well and was always ambitious with what I wanted for my future but I can happily state that God has far exceeded my achievements in comparison to what I believed myself able to achieve. I love children so I knew I wanted to be a good mother to my own and this involved doing things that I knew they would enjoy, basically I did the opposite of what I saw my parents had done. A great sense of passion started to build in me whilst working with children and families. As a result, training to be a Probation Officer became part of my journey which led to my first Degree.

As God elevated me within my career I continued to study and learn new things, I remember feeling petrified when I applied to do my Master's. I originally applied to do Social Enterprise but this course was cancelled due to not enough applicants so I studied Psychology instead. I was determined to improve myself educationally and although it took a while I did achieve my Master's and celebrated my graduation with my 2 adult children. I do believe that it was the rejection and neglect from my family that caused me to take a different route for my own life's journey.

People's rejection is Gods protection, I love this saying because it is so true and is a definitely applies to many parts of my journey.

Nurture

BEAUTY IS THE OPPOSITE OF PERFECTION— IT'S ABOUT CONFIDENCE, CHARISMA AND CHARACTER.

The discovery that the outside world is indeed the brain's real food is truly intriguing. The brain gobbles up its external environment in bits and chunks through its sensory system, vision, hearing, smell and taste. Kotulak (1993) The Nurture side of the Nature vs. Nurture debate explains human behaviour by examining socialization, environment, and relationships, moving away from biology and evolution. When a girl child is born, her family will usually socialize her to be feminized. They will grow her hair, clothe her in dresses, buy dolls, all conforming their child to the feminine ideal before the child has any idea of what gender is. This is referred to as gender socialization. It is also valuable to examine an individual's social environment when considering their behaviour.

Sociologists believe social environments, interactions, and structures shape human behaviour. Family types, family structures, subcultures, media, government, wealth, and inequality all mould an individual's personality which ultimately drives their behaviour. Philosophers Jean-Jacques Rousseau and John Locke independently thought that people are born as blank slates and that their eventual individual differences develop solely due to the result of environmental influences (Psychology Encyclopaedia, 2017; Duschinsky, 2012; Nesterak, 2015).

Twentieth century behavioural psychologist John Watson shared a similar perspective, believing that the events that take place during early childhood have far more influence on what kind of adults we become compared to the effects of our genes (Haggbloom et al, 2002). The research does indicate that environment is stronger than genes.

I will explore this using my own life timeline. I was born the last out of 5 children born to my mother, I also came 5 years following my brother's birth whilst all other siblings were born within 12 months of each other, 2 actually born within the same year, putting them very close in age. I do not remember much about my early days up to 2 years old but was told my father was violent to my mother and to my siblings. I do remember standing at the bottom of the stairs of my first house when I was about a year old and looking up where I saw what looked like a bird walking at the top of the stairs. I remember being very frightened by this and screamed for my parents to come and get me as I was outside the front room door, I think they may have accidently locked me out, that is the last memory I have from this house.

We subsequently moved from the South West to another house in the East when I was 2 years old, I remember a lot more from then. My mother left me with numerous child-minders but recalls I never liked staying with them and cried all the time so she had to give up work to be with me. Whilst reflecting back, I remember being with these child-minders and actually enjoying it and can still remember about 4 of them and some of the things I used to do such as eating mash potato and spaghetti, another child minder had a tortoise that I was a little scared of.

I remember I wore a nice pink party dress for my second or third birthday, apparently I also had a party but do not remember that, I only remember the dress and also telling my brother he could not have any of my chocolate. This was a family joke for some time. My step-father and my mother would fight all the time, he would hit her and also would hit my siblings, and we spent many nights walking the streets looking for somewhere to sleep because of this. This was

91

pretty much my childhood, there was no comfort, cuddles, toys or anyone that cuddled me or comforted me. I became self-sufficient and developed survival skills that provided for my basic needs, such as my food and clothes. I remember coming in from playing outside to often no dinner, everyone had finished their food and there was none left for me. My mother would say she 'forgot' about me. I used this opportunity to get chips and a saveloy which I actually preferred (I did not like my mother's cooking). I was able to enjoy this type of meal from the local fish and chip shop most evenings. I had no real sense of belonging but tried to fit within the family structure, although this was hard and eventually I gave up because it seemed pointless and was hurtful to be ignored. Once my step-father had finally left the house I was further alienated, probably because I was branded as his favourite and now he was gone, it was probably their way of payback. I recall us getting cats, I found comfort and closeness with one of my cats and I suppose this was a place I started to form cuddles and a sense of love, I still love cats today and find them extremely therapeutic to the point I had 2 cats as an adult for 17 years.

I also found comfort lying down on the bed with my eldest sister who would always rock at the end of the bed to music, at the time nobody realized her rocking was due to trauma and an indication she was severely disturbed, the family just saw this as her thing that she did to music, I found comfort in the rocking. I guess this was my way of feeling the rocking effect without actually doing it, it was another sense of comfort for me and was very soothing. I learnt at a very young age that any comfort and closeness I experienced was something I had to find for myself, it was not given or willingly provided.

This, I guess interfered with the attachment process for me.

However, when I explore the different stages below of attachment areas of secure, resistant, avoidance, surprisingly, I do believe my character as an adult is more in line with the psychologist Mary Ainsworth secure attachment framework but this has taken a lot of hard work.

	Stage 1: Attachment	Stage 2: Independence	Stage 3: Achievement	Stage 4: Altruism
Secure	Friendship Cooperation Intimacy Respect Trust Love	Self-control Confident Assertive Responsible Autonomous	Successful Problem solver Creative Resilient Persistent Motivated	Caring Compassion Empathy
Resistant	Attention-seeking Crave affection Clinging	Rebellious Reckless Manipulative Bullies Passive Aggressive	Over achiever Workaholic Delinquent skills Cheating Overly competitive Risk seeking	Selfish Over Indulgent Co-dependent Self-abasing
Avoidant	Alienation Withdrawn Rejected Lonely Suspicious	Look confident Learned helplessness Easily misled Lacks self-control Irresponsible	Under achiever Failure oriented Unmotivated Lazy Avoids risks Fears change Immature	Narcissistic Hedonistic Anti-social Psychopathic Exploitative

The reason for this is I do believe the attachment which is stage 1 reflects a little of avoidance and resistance but when exploring stage 2 Independence, stage 3 Achievement and stage 4 Altruism, I do believe I am mostly in the secure section but this could also be because I do not really allow anyone to get too close to me. When I am in a relationship I can be rebellious, crave attention and become suspicious. Although I have a great sense of self control, I am assertive, responsible, autonomous, motivated, resilient, persistent, a problem solver, successful in my own right, caring and compassionate.

At this point I have to give the glory for this to God, my heavenly Father, through Jesus Christ my saviour who died for me. When I decided to give my life to God I realized through Christ he actually was the one who gave his life to and for me but what really made a difference for me was knowing I am loved and feeling that love.

I also believe that being introduced to God from a young age left an imprint that he was good which subsequently led me on a journey which has been hard but fruitful and certainly, at times empowering. I believe this type of introduction had a nurturing aspect from young that not even I was aware of. During my first experiences of church, I observed mental illness from my mother and people treating someone I loved and cared for badly so the imprint for me was people who go to church are hypocrites and uncaring, the scriptures I read about was about love and kindness. However, I did not experience this as a child and so kept away from church places until I needed to get my children into a church school, it was here my journey began…

Although I have still come across hypocrisy within church walls, it was not as severe as what I experienced as a child. I mostly focus on how I behave towards others but also choose churches where it feels right and where people are welcoming and caring. I do feel my childhood environment has had an effect on me and would be lying if I stated it didn't but I know I *do not look like where I came from*. This is a saying for people who have accomplished outside the 'box' of their life.

People sometimes place others in a box stating if they do not come from a particular background they are not able to achieve above this invisible threshold created by the oppressors and ignorance. I mentioned this earlier on in my book when I met with a Christian counsellor which is what he called himself. I think we have to believe people can advance beyond the expectations society can place them regardless of where they are from or what childhood environment they were brought up in.

However, I do believe that sustaining it and maintaining success can be harder to achieve when you have not had the 'training 'and opportunities that some may have had if coming from a secure environment. I know I am ambitious, I know I am determined and focused and feel blessed for the achievements I have made. Although this is the case, I have struggled to maintain this, mostly because it has taken a lot of hard work and sacrifice but also because I have had no role models or anything that looked similar to where I am going or want to go. I remember feeling suicidal following my daughters first birthday when no one in my family attended. I was scared and believed I could not be the mother she needed me to be because where I was coming from, my history was full of a family that never quite made it mentally and thought Leanne would be better off without me. I had everything for my fate planned but God had other plans for me. Thankfully, this thought was disrupted when I started to wonder that if I was not around, who would be there for Leanne. If my family were not supportive to me during my time of sadness then how would they treat my daughter, would they look after her well? I asked myself all of these questions but did not feel confident that they would.

The next thing I knew I was on a train travelling to see James not knowing what the outcome would be, petrified that I was making a terrible mistake due to his history of violence but somehow the place where I was mentally was far worse than anything he done or could do to me. The positives were that he and his family did welcome Leanne and I, even if it was for a short while and for his own selfish reasons and even though it never worked out, I know now that it was not supposed to work out but was one of God's many interventions in my life that I believe actually literally saved my life and protected me from making a more serious mistake.

Nature

The most prominent nature explanation of human behaviour is that humans, as animals act according to their primal instincts. This view is held by many biologists and some branches of psychology e.g. evolutionary psychology. Charles Darwin was born in1809, he died in 1882. His famous quotes include: "Owing to this struggle for life, any variation, however slight and from whatever cause proceeding, if it be in any degree profitable to an individual of any species, in its infinitely complex relationship to other organic beings and to external nature, will tend to the preservation of that individual, and will generally be inherited by its offspring. Psychologist Sir Francis Galton in 1869 described the impact of genes and biology versus environmental influences.

Many others have debated these theories since Hippocrates was alive. Around 400 B.C.E., Hippocrates described human behaviours as being biological, the result of four different body fluid types called humours. This was, Yellow bile, Blood, Black bile and Phlegm. While certain physical traits like skin and eye colour have been found to be the result of direct genetic inheritance, virtually any pattern of thinking or behaviour can be understood from the perspective of a combination of nature and nurture.

In the animal kingdom, domestication of many species is understood to be the result of encouraging domesticated behaviours (nurture), then having animals that most successfully adopt those behaviours breed with each other so it becomes part of their nature (Bouchard, 1994).

In humans, the question of nature vs. nurture somewhat continues to be debated concerning human behaviour, intelligence, and in the development of personality traits (Psychology Encyclopaedia, 2017).

As with most human traits, intelligence is now understood to be the result of some combination of both nature and nurture. While genes have a great influence on the size and biochemistry of the brain, its full development does not usually occur until after the first 20 years of life. Also, the heredity of intelligence tends to vary between different aspects of cognition. I do believe the natural element of my life, the biological genes that is fixed and part of my DNA has been crucial and does dictate within my character and ambitions. I also believe, I along with everyone else, have a uniqueness that has been developed and shaped as a result my own life experiences.

As mentioned, I am the youngest of my siblings but never felt part of the family unit, it always felt as though I entered into the family at an inconvenience. My mother had an affair and I was born as a result of this. My mother spent most of my childhood telling me 'I would die young' although this was hard to hear as mentioned but I often wonder if this is why she did not invest or show any belief in me. If she thought I was not going to be around for long, she probably thought there was no point. My siblings were all very close in age two born in the same year so they practically grew up almost like triplets together.

The home environment was abusive so there was a lot of brokenness when I arrived, I was then exposed to my step-fathers violence towards my mother and my siblings. Although they all said he was not violent towards me only when he hit me when I accidently broke his cigarette when I was about 8, the blow he gave me across my head was so hard all I could hear was a ringing sound and a throbbing, muffled silence. I was extremely scared and quickly ran to the outside toilet where no one could get in if locked from the inside. I felt safe there for what felt like hours until I thought he had calmed down. however, it was just as traumatic to see others being subjected to his violence. He was also sexually abusive towards me at a very young age, although this was never really acknowledged... I do believe that if he was allowed to stay in the house following the time he broke my sister's arm, he probably would have used more physical and sexual abuse towards me.

I also believe he probably knew I was not his biological child, although he never said it, I think deep down, he knew the truth because he did treat me differently according to my mother and siblings. However, he did not spare me from his molestation. This abuse was horrific and subsequently led me to promiscuous behaviour from a young age. However, I managed to have what I consider to be a long-term relationship which is an accomplishment considering I was a teenager. I believe this relationship, if only 3 years (on and off) really helped me understand that I preferred long-term than short term relationship's even though I was not aware of this at the time.

I know I have the ability to sustain a form of closeness with the opposite sex, especially as at the time my peers were not sustaining their relationships for as long. Although, I was able to have this and enjoyed it at the time, I now know through Christ, I am looking forward to sustaining a more mature connection one day, which is much more meaningful and positive.

Although, I did not observe or have any feelings of warmth and love between my parents, from my parents or even my siblings. I do believe in love and family, I always seek to understand what it means to me, so could this be because it's more instinctual. I suppose it is probably common to imagine what the absent biological parent might be like but without knowing the truth it is hard to make comparisons. When thinking about my mother's heritage, I know she grew up separate from her parents and came to London at the age of 19 years old where she not long after met my Step-father.

Whilst there was a family value, admittedly my step-father also grew up separate from his parents but when he came to London he had family already there, most of my stepfathers side of family are high achievers in comparison to mothers side. In relation to this, it would be difficult to link my achievements or ambitious habits with my stepfather as we are not biologically related, neither did I have a close relationship with his side of family because it seemed they looked down on us, they always kept their distance. This would also rule out any form of nurturing that may have formed or developed from environment.

I have always wanted to achieve something, whether it was to get the prize in school for attending the most days or doing well in my spelling test to learning to drive or getting a qualification. I enjoy studying and learning something new, I can be a risk taker who navigates into new environments that take me out of my comfort zone. Although this is uncomfortable at first, somehow I have a high resilience and a strong determination that enables me to push through regardless of the discomfort.

There is a natural element to who I am that does not look like where I came from, my ambitions, determination and sense of family values does not mirror what I experienced growing up in my home environment. I can never be certain that I have more of my biological fathers genes neither can I be sure there are any similarities because I have never met him or any of his family but equally, I have never been able to find much similarities with my mother's family either which is why I can't help but explore the possibilities using the nature versus nurture debate. However, just like flowers, without a natural habitat and a nurturing environment, it would be hard for them to grow constructively.

'He has made everything beautiful in its time, he has also set eternity in the human heart, yet no one can fathom what God has done from beginning to end' Ecclesiastes 3:11. Henry Stapp, a quantum physicist and mathematician, believes each person who understands him or herself in this way, as a spark of the divine, with some small part of the divine power integrally interwoven into the process of the creation of the psycho-physical universe, will be encouraged to participate in the process of plumbing the potentialities, and shaping the form of, the unfolding quantum reality that is his or her birth right to help create.

Dr Caroline Leaf also researched the science of thought and mind-body connection as it relates to thinking, learning and emotions. I had the pleasure to hear her speak about her research at a conference. She believes when we recognise the unique power that is in our minds, 'plumbing the depths of our divine nature' will become a revelation of our sense of worth as human beings. It will enable us to love ourselves and, in turn, love others as we acknowledge the divine spark that is in them as well. Leaf (2017) These views and concepts have helped strengthen my faith and belief that when God created the blueprint for the universe, I and every one of us, were already part of the plan. Science and scriptures consistently evidence we are all unique in our own individual way which is brilliantly designed to fill a role no one else can. I also believe that the more I continue to believe in myself and function in my truth, the more fulfilling and impactful my life will become.

Very truly, we speak of what we know and we testify to what we have seen. John 3:11

Flowers – My Bed Of Roses

So nature and nurture are both important when it comes to the baby growing brain they work in tandem, with genes providing the building blocks and the environment acting like an on the job foreman, providing instructions for final construction experiences like little carpenters all can quickly change the architecture of the brain and sometimes they can turn into vandals. I noticed I started to achieve success when I became an adult and left to live in a new area with my children. One can say this was due to a new environment but this is probably not the case because it was just that, it was new. I believe it is a possibility that it is partly my strong genes that allowed me to be able to flourish and the fact that I moved to a more constructive environment that gave me the freedom to be myself but mostly because of my faith and trust in Jesus Christ that has enabled me to cope and build a constructive system within myself that has helped sustain me.

My bed of roses is my last chapter because of the phrase 'life is not a bed of roses' the expression a bed of roses came into use as an idiom in the 1500s and is still used today. I want to use this expression in a positive way because I love flowers and I have based my life journey within this book describing the growth of a flower from the earth. I believe my life started in an environment where one might not expect there to be any achievements or success.

This I mirrored with a plant that does not have good soil or if it does not get watered or care, it will either die or after a while you will see wild weeds growing.

This can be disappointing because now something is growing but not what was intended. I see life like this, if we fail to get the necessary care, love and support needed, we too can become like wild unintentional weeds sprouting, with an uncertainty about life and many questions about who we are which also raised questions for me about who God is. Although I have had some experiences that have left me broken and with the need to fight for survival, like a knot wild weed that takes over areas where the soil has been disturbed.

However, I realized when I became born again through Christ that area of me died but the unattractive dead canes remained left behind. It took years for these to be broken down from my mindset, soul, behaviour, identity and attitude because I now base all these on Jesus Christ and through his blood that was shed for me. It is through understanding this sacrifice I have found a renewed strength, perception and courage to face my life's journey. I am also using this to help me establish love and forgiveness which I am still working through. I am a working progress and so is life, understanding life has a turbulence that if you are not rooted in a discipline you can get carried away as easy as bits of pollen blowing in the wind.

My discipline incorporates prayer, fasting, kindness, worship, Bible Scripture study and reflection. I do not have an end date or a goal according to my faith other than getting to know my God through Jesus Christ better today than I did yesterday.

I started my book with earth, this was from the time I was born but thankfully God knew me before I was born.

Jeremiah 1 v 5: I knew you before I formed you in the womb

He set me apart and I was always his.

I know this now so it did not matter that the soil became spoilt because God also created the heaven and the earth. My next area was seeds, many seeds fell and I will try and define this using a scripture.

Matthew 13: A farmer went out to sow his seed, as he was scattered the seed, and some fell on rocky places, where it did not have much soil. It sprang up quickly, because the soil was shallow. But when the sun came up, the plants were scorched, and they withered because they had no root. Still other seed fell on good soil, where it produced a crop—a hundred, sixty or thirty times what was sown.

This scripture represents the word of God and how we can miss the meaning if we are not careful but I also relate this to my beginning of life.

I do feel that some of the things that happened to me as a child was like a seed that did not take root inside of me, although the seed sprang up quickly the soil was damaged so when the sunlight came up the plants was scorched and withered in the sun because there was no root. I believe it is God's plan to not allow certain seeds to take root in our lives but to allow the seeds he knows to be good for us take root. I realized that this may not look like what we expect because what we perceive as 'good seeds' may be very different from what God has in store for us. I believe I had good and bad seeds that took root and it was allowed to be formed and grew together. This always reminded me of where I came from but also gave me determination and strength to strive towards something that was better.

The plume emerges and nodes for me relates to my journey throughout teenage and early adult years. I felt as though I was having to catch up on the years I missed.

I had an opportunity when I left to live alone to try and be all the things I wanted to achieve but my expectations were quite low in comparison to the achievements I made and continue to make. It was not just about academic achievements it was also about finding a self-worth and understanding who I was as a girl and then as a women.

During my school years was what really helped to create a core in me, I learnt a lot of my life skills which helped me form an identity and shape character during this time. I believe this was the way the lord sprinkled good seeds with sunshine into my life, it was a safe environment, a place where I could accomplish goals, get recognition with praise, learn about relationships and working with others but mostly it provided consistency and routine. This was a contrast to my home life and is and will always be a very valuable time in my life.

It has helped me to realize that schools are not just educational establishments for children they have the opportunity to provide a lot more than they realize especially for those who experience neglect or abuse in their home environment.

I enjoyed school and soaked up all they had to offer but can acknowledge that this is not always the same for all children who come from dysfunctional home environments. A childhood friend recently told me another girl who we went to school with was consistently sexually abused by her step father as a child, I recall her always being unwell and being off school, I even remember the day she fainted whilst at school.

This suggests we all can display the effects of childhood abuse differently. Unfortunately for her, when she told her mother as an adult they refused to believe her and sadly the rest of her family stopped speaking to her... I was sorry to hear this but could also relate to her pain of not receiving support. My teenage years was exciting but also very difficult because I had some very painful experiences that has left me with a very cautious approach to others especially men. My siblings were very different from me but come to think of it they were also different from each other in relation to their interests but visibly shared a sense of belonging between each other that was evident in the unspoken abuse they had all experienced, although, they did not acknowledge the abuse I was subjected to.

This made me different, I stood out and was abandoned to the corner stone of the family unit. This was and is a lonely place to be but it made me self-sufficient and resilient. I spent my teenage years outside of the house, I had a group of friends that were probably not really friends but people who I felt a connection with. I had a lot of fun with them and they served a great purpose for me because I had no one. Due to my embarrassment and loyalty to my family I did not really share the true abandonment I felt to anyone but it became very apparent to Neil my boyfriend because I would always stay at his house and no one ever came looking for me or showed any interest in my whereabouts. I believe he was aware of just how alone I really was, he also knew about my pain, so I guess this helped to bring us closer together in an awkward but enduring way. That's probably why he always came back when I ended the relationship and this happened weekly.

It became our 'thing' it was like the protocol to our relationship. Neil knew he would always mess up and I knew he would always come back or attempt to come back until one day he could not come back because he was sent to prison. This changed the course and dynamics of our relationship. Following his departure I spent a few years living in hostels and this helped me to start to get to know myself and make positive changes. I do believe the appearance of nodes in my life was a reflection of some of the people and things that helped me along the way but as mentioned there were weeds that also remained and these weeds I believe were people that did not continue with me on my life journey and still remain absent. The stems and petals relate to my achievements and success, I do not know what the next chapter of life will look like, or how my journey will continue to unfold, but whilst I continue my path of trust and faith in my heavenly father, I believe the rest of my story will be just as it should be. I heard some wise words from a very gracious and articulate person. 'Your story is what you have, what you will always have. It is something you own' Michelle Obama, 2018. These encouraging words propel me to continue to rise above the ashes and soiling of what was, to be enabled, renewed and liberated with a sense of ownership, whilst adding to my story and hopefully administer a sense of hope and possibility to others in the process. As you now know, my life has been no bed of roses but I do feel through the withered weeds God managed to allow some flowers to bloom and he continues to do this in my life.

Isaiah 35:1: The desert and the parched land will be glad; the wilderness will rejoice and blossom as the crocus (flower)

END

I have written this book in memory of my brother 1965-1999, I believe he has gone to a better place but is truly missed. May he RIEP

A special thanks to Surrender the Secrets series, which enabled a group of five incredible women whom I have never met but who helped to take me on a personal journey to receive forgiveness, healing and restoration. Nobody tells you about the real costs that follow having an abortion. The sorrow, the brokenness and pain that you can carry around with you, and the impact of this on your life following what is perceived as 'a procedure'.

Thanks to Cecil Stokes, Jill, Jane, Courtney, Vanessa, and Kelly. Your courage and commitment to this very important topic is beyond amazing and certainly helped me understand the truth which alleviated pain that longed to be acknowledged, resulting in a new found hope.

Isaiah 60:20. Thy sun shall no more go down, neither shall thy moon withdraw itself, for the Lord will be thine everlasting light, and the days of thy mourning shall be ended.